HESBURGH OF NOTRE DAME

PRAISE FOR

Hesburgh of Notre Dame: The Church's Public Intellectual

"This study of the remarkable multifaceted career of Theodore Hesburgh provides an illuminating perspective on the too-little-studied role of the public intellectual in the United States."

—*Mary Ann Glendon*
Learned Hand Professor of Law, Harvard University

"Fr. Hesburgh's contributions to church and state are extraordinary by any standard, and this new book by Todd Ream inspires even as it explains. A thoroughly enjoyable and moving testament of a priest whose story deserves to be told and retold."

—*Rev. Dennis H. Holtschneider, CM*
President, Association of Catholic Colleges and Universities

"Ream has written an outstanding book about an outstanding life. As a leader in Christian higher education, I am interested in what shapes the life of a university president and how each is called to use the role as a platform of influence inside and outside of the university. Father Hesburgh's thirty-five-year tenure allowed him to be involved in almost all of the major conversations that were occurring during his leadership tenure. Ream carefully covers Hesburgh's writings on immigration, the Peace Corps, and civil rights, to name just a few. At all times it is clear that Father Hesburgh's identity as a person of deeply committed Christian faith is at the core of his being and of his service as a public intellectual, a type of influence we need now from the academy. All of the issues Hesburgh addressed remain—refugees and asylum seekers, international peacemaking, and the eradication of racism. Protestants, Catholics, and any leader in the public square will benefit from Hesburgh's timeless wisdom captured so thoroughly and ably by Ream."

—*Shirley V. Hoogstra*
President, Council for Christian Colleges and Universities

"In various forms, much has been written and recorded about the remarkable life of my brother in Holy Cross, mentor and friend, Father Ted Hesburgh. What makes Todd Ream's work different is his deep exploration into the theological and philosophical foundations of Father Hesburgh's life as a public intellectual in service to God, country, and Notre Dame."

—*Rev. John I. Jenkins, CSC*
President, University of Notre Dame

"Father Hesburgh was a towering voice for justice who sacrificed on behalf of so many people over the course of his life. *Hesburgh of Notre Dame* is an eloquent introduction to Father Hesburgh's rightful place as the Church's public intellectual and a truly great figure of the twentieth century."

—*John M. Perkins*
Co-Founder, Christian Community Development Association

"Whatever one's convictions about faith, education, and politics may be, one will likely agree that Theodore M. Hesburgh was one of the great Christian educators and public intellectuals of the twentieth century. This book is a wonderful introduction to his person and vision, especially for those who, like me, have followed Father Hesburgh's work only from afar."

—*Miroslav Volf*
Henry B. Wright Professor of Systematic Theology and Director of
the Yale Center for Faith and Culture, Yale University

HESBURGH OF NOTRE DAME

THE CHURCH'S PUBLIC INTELLECTUAL

Todd C. Ream

Foreword by Leon E. Panetta

Paulist Press

New York / Mahwah, NJ

Cover image: University of Notre Dame Archives (GMDG-23-06-01)—Portrait of Rev. Theodore M. Hesburgh at Commencement, 1981
Cover design by Mark Lo Bello
Book design by Lynn Else

Library of Congress Cataloging-in-Publication Data
Names: Ream, Todd C., author.
Title: Hesburgh of Notre Dame : the Church's public intellectual / Todd C. Ream ; foreword by Leon E. Panetta.
Description: New York : Paulist Press, 2021. | Includes index. | Summary: "An informative resource concerning the historical significance of Fr. Hesburgh's life, the efforts he made, and the challenges he faced"— Provided by publisher.
Identifiers: LCCN 2020006873 (print) | LCCN 2020006874 (ebook) | ISBN 9780809154029 (paperback) | ISBN 9781587687808 (ebook)
Subjects: LCSH: Hesburgh, Theodore M. (Theodore Martin), 1917-2015. | University of Notre Dame—Presidents—Biography.
Classification: LCC LD4112.7.H47 R43 2021 (print) | LCC LD4112.7.H47 (ebook) | DDC 378.772/89--dc23
LC record available at https://lccn.loc.gov/2020006873
LC ebook record available at https://lccn.loc.gov/2020006874

ISBN 978-0-8091-5402-9 (paperback)
ISBN 978-1-58768-780-8 (e-book)

Published by Paulist Press
997 Macarthur Boulevard
Mahwah, New Jersey 07430
www.paulistpress.com

Printed and bound in the
United States of America

In memory of my grandparents
With Father Hesburgh,
Harlow and Caroline Ream,
and
William and Esther Taylor
Part of the Greatest Generation

CONTENTS

FOREWORD

LEON E. PANETTA
Former Secretary of Defense, CIA Director,
and Chairman of the Panetta Institute

Father Theodore Hesburgh was one of the nation's most influential leaders in higher education, the Catholic Church, and national and international affairs.

He was the fifteenth president of the University of Notre Dame from 1952 until his retirement in 1987, ending the longest tenure among active presidents of American colleges and universities.

Father Hesburgh served four popes and held sixteen presidential appointments that involved him in virtually all major social issues— civil rights, peaceful uses of atomic energy, campus unrest, treatment of Vietnam draft evaders, and Third World development and immigration reform.

But Father Ted, as he was known to the students of Notre Dame, was first and foremost a priest, a servant of God, who deeply believed in the dignity of all people and their right to a better life. His lifelong commitment was to justice for all.

He was a charter member of the U.S. Commission on Civil Rights, created in 1957, and he chaired the commission from 1969 to 1972. When I was Director of the U.S. Office for Civil Rights, the agency dedicated to promoting equal education for all children, I met with Father Hesburgh and we both strongly supported the enforcement of civil rights laws. We both lost our jobs because the Nixon Administration had made a commitment to the so-called Southern strategy, which promised a slowdown in civil rights enforcement. President Nixon replaced Father Hesburgh as chairman of the commission, and I lost my job as director. I was always proud of the fact that this Jesuit-trained son of Italian immigrants had stood with the President of Notre Dame in fighting for equal justice for all.

That was Father Ted's legacy in all that he accomplished. He was a member of President Ford's Presidential Clemency Board charged with deciding the fate of various groups of Vietnam offenders. His work on these commissions led to the creation at Notre Dame Law School of the Center of Civil and Human Rights.

Between 1979 and 1981 he chaired the Select Commission on Immigration and Refugee Policy, the recommendations of which became the basis of Congressional reform legislation five years later that I worked on as a member of Congress. He was involved during the 1980s in a private initiative that sought to unite internationally known scientists and world religious leaders in condemning nuclear weapons. His global leadership was the impetus for the establishment at Notre Dame of the Kellogg Institute for International Studies and the Kroc Institute for International Peace Studies.

He was the permanent Vatican City representative to the International Atomic Energy Agency in Vienna from 1956 to 1970. In 1972, at the request of Pope Paul VI, he built the Ecumenical Institute at Tantur, Jerusalem. He was the head of the Vatican representatives attending the twentieth anniversary of the United Nations human rights declaration in Teheran, Iran, in 1968.

Father Hesburgh was a national leader in the field of education, serving on many commissions and study groups. As an example, he served as chairman of the International Federation of Catholic Universities from 1963 to 1970 and led a movement to redefine the nature and mission of the Catholic university.

His stature as an elder statesman in American higher education is reflected in his 150 honorary degrees, the most ever awarded to one person, and he was the first person from higher education to be awarded the Congressional Gold Medal and the nation's highest civilian honor—the Medal of Freedom.

As a former Secretary of Defense, I was honored that the Navy made him an Honorary Chaplain in 2013, fulfilling in part his dream from seventy years earlier of serving as chaplain aboard an aircraft carrier.

He truly was the Church's public intellectual. But throughout his many national and international accomplishments, he remained Father Ted—a priest committed to doing everything possible to improve the lives of all people. This book is a wonderful reflection of all that Father Hesburgh accomplished. Yet for those of us who knew him and worked with him, he will be remembered not just as an intellectual, but as a priest and a patriot committed to God, country, and Notre Dame.

ACKNOWLEDGMENTS

Over time, I have turned with greater speed and interest to acknowledgments sections. A large part of my reason for doing so was the realization that authoring books taught me several lessons, chief among them that no scholarly effort is definitive, nor is any such effort the creation of a single person. Those sections thus became personalized confirmations of those lessons and windows into why authors commit themselves to particular projects. I hope what follows offers the same for you.

Since first writing a paper on Father Hesburgh while a graduate student over twenty years ago, I believed more needed to be written about him and, in particular, more needed to be written about what animated him. Although impressive in their own ways, the books I was finding seemed incomplete. Little did I understand, however, that those perceptions were not solely the result of my own intellectual inspiration. In contrast, those perceptions were the result of the ways a plethora of individuals instilled within me an inclination to first consider what was theologically at stake when exploring a figure such as Hesburgh and, in turn, what virtues were needed in order to rightly conduct such an exploration.

Those lessons were the result of the interactions I was privileged to share with my parents, Charles and Linda Ream, as well as my grandparents, Harlow and Carolyn Ream and William and Esther Taylor. Over the years, teachers such as Steve Benke, Winfred Moore, Dennis Campbell, Lee Upcraft, and J. R. Weaver also implicitly made their own contributions to the shape and focus of this project.

Most recently, the shape and focus of this project came as a result of insights offered by Donna Crilly, Senior Academic Editor at Paulist Press. Initially, I naïvely came to her with an idea for a comprehensive biography of Father Hesburgh as a first effort (a project that I now believe is all the more needed but which I was not prepared to pursue at that time). Knowing the literature needed an accessible introduction and that such an effort would allow me to refine how I theologically understood Hesburgh, she wisely suggested the book in its present form. Donna was also willing to extend patience when it became apparent on more than one occasion that I was not going to meet our agreed-upon deadlines. Instead of viewing such challenges as shameful, Donna graciously redirected my thinking about them as opportunities to refine my thinking about Hesburgh. While missing deadlines is not a practice I now endorse, those instances, as Donna indicated, improved the quality of this project.

Several members of the larger Notre Dame community also graciously offered their wisdom concerning Father Hesburgh and thus, in turn, refined my own. First and foremost, Father Hesburgh's youngest sibling and brother, James, shared his insights with me. Through him, for example, I first learned why the efforts made by Andean Health and Development were so important to his brother. James Hesburgh then introduced me to his daughter, Maureen Ryan, who added in considerable ways to my understanding.

I believe that being an evangelical allows me to recognize components of Father Hesburgh's identity as a Catholic priest and member of the Congregation of Holy Cross that others may find commonplace and thus not notice. However, that subtle yet (I hope) charitable distance also meant that I needed to immerse myself into Father Hesburgh's world in ways that might not prove necessary for others. To that end, priests of the Congregation of Holy Cross such as Father Austin Collins (the Religious Superior of Holy Cross Priests and Brothers at Notre Dame and a Professor of Sculpture), Father Tom Blantz (Professor of History Emeritus), Father Wilson Miscamble (Professor of History), and Father Gerard Olinger (Vice President for Mission

Acknowledgments

Engagement and Church Affairs) became invaluable and thus much-appreciated conversation partners.

Notre Dame's Cushwa Center for the Study of American Catholicism provides scholars with an amazing array of opportunities for intellectual community and support. Such opportunities are the result of the vision its director, Kathleen Sprows Cummings, has cultivated for the center and the way her colleagues such as Shane Ulbrich, the center's assistant director, tirelessly labor alongside her to bring that vision to fruition. Despite the demands on his time, Shane answered countless questions and provided advice on a wide range of matters pertaining to Father Hesburgh's legacy. Philip Byers, a former student, friend, a PhD candidate in American religious history at Notre Dame, and now a research associate with the Cushwa Center, also brought to my attention several resources concerning Father Hesburgh that I otherwise would have missed.

Marty Ogren, Father Hesburgh's former driver, and Patrick Borders from the president's office, each allowed me to spend time in Father Hesburgh's office as I thought through the books and images with which he surrounded himself. Among many other lessons, these experiences confirmed how influential Jacques Maritain's writings were on Father Hesburgh. As this book notes, Maritain's influence was arguably woven into Hesburgh's speeches more than any other philosopher or theologian. Not surprisingly, marked copies of Maritain's books were present in greater numbers in Hesburgh's office than the works of any other scholar. In addition, they were shelved in a prominent position next to "Father Hesburgh's Window," the window that looked from his thirteenth-floor office in the library now bearing his name (or "Touchdown Jesus" to football fans) toward the Basilica of the Sacred Heart and the main building atop which stands the famed nine-foot, four-thousand-pound, gold-leaf-covered statue of the university's namesake—Notre Dame du Lac or Our Lady of the Lake.

As previously echoed, several secondary sources influenced the ideas in this book. To rectify the perceived deficiency in the literature, however, I focused my efforts with greatest intent on Hesburgh's own words and, in particular, words found in his speeches. While often more incomplete than his published articles and books, his speeches provide the most apt opportunity to understand the development of his thinking and to do so in relation to a wide variety of topics. I thus leaned heavily on efforts made by the archivists at Notre Dame. Joseph Smith filled countless requests for documents and images, while Charles Lamb and William Kevin Cawley helped me focus and, at times, even correct my thinking. This project would obviously not have been possible without them.

Evelyn Bence, freelance editor extraordinaire, not only helped refine my writing but thought to question details such as whether the Basilica of the Sacred Heart was a basilica at the time of Father Hesburgh's ordination. She thus kept me from making any number of mistakes I will keep to myself as I fear no excuses exist for me having made them.

With the Lumen Research Institute, Jerry Pattengale and Chris Devers are constant sources of encouragement. They ask about work and take an interest in Father Hesburgh's life and legacy. However, they never fail to ask the truly important questions, such as ones regarding the well-being of family. They help one do the best work possible but also keep life in perspective. For their friendship, I am truly grateful.

At Taylor University, I am fortunate to call Bill Ringenberg, Tom Jones, and Ben Wetzel friends and colleagues. On one level, our lunchtime conversations are an interpersonal highlight of each week. On another level, their training as historians and particularly as Americanists keeps me honest in my appraisals of various matters. Their influence not only enhanced this project but, in many ways kept me out of any number of patches of weeds into which I might have otherwise found myself tempted to wander.

One of the most impressive components of dedicating one's life to teaching is when former students become colleagues and friends. Two of the most impressive and gracious students with whom I was privileged to work, Hannah Adderley Pick (now at the University of

Acknowledgments

Portland) and Julia VanderMolen (now at Calvin University), read the manuscript and offered considerable suggestions. Both came to Taylor University with abilities defying disciplinary boundaries, and fortunately we in no way diminished those abilities during their time on campus. To no one's surprise, both penned theses of the highest distinction in their respective classes. They also wisely challenged me to see Hesburgh in his full complexity.

I have had the privilege of working with Erin Drummy as a research associate for the last two and a half years. A graduate program will soon be very fortunate to welcome her as a member of its entering class of students. While at Taylor, Erin read several works concerning Father Hesburgh and coauthored a chapter concerning public intellectuals for *Higher Education: Handbook of Theory and Research*. Along with a related book, she read this manuscript in full and made suggestions that greatly contributed to its value.

Andrew Deskins, my closest friend since our days in graduate school, also read the manuscript and offered considerable suggestions. On an almost weekly basis, he indulges me in some "Father Ted-talk" and has also helped me over the years to refine my thinking. Much to my chagrin, those conversations often take place over the phone rather than around a campfire in Montana. When retirement comes, perhaps we will find ourselves there with far greater frequency and no longer in need of technology to maintain our friendship.

My wife, Sara, shares a place in my heart that transcends friendship and for which I am eternally grateful. She graciously accepted Father Ted as a fifth member of our family and, for example, managed to summon considerable excitement in Patrick Creadon's *Hesburgh* documentary when it was released on DVD in September 2019. While she has only watched it once (at least to my knowledge), I would not be surprised if she was equally excited if someone she knows well suggested that we watch it again. She not only read each chapter as it was drafted, but then she also read the whole manuscript. As always, she helped me discern the mystery of a well-placed comma while also not collapsing into some theologically suspect line of thinking.

Our daughters, Addison and Ashley, also accepted Father Ted as a fifth member of our family and have managed to do so with far greater grace than I would have when I was a teenager. Part of my hope in terms of such a project is to influence the generation of leaders—educational, ecclesial, political, or otherwise—that will play roles in the lives of my daughters and members of their generation. To inflate our own sense of importance, my contemporaries and I have exaggerated the challenges presently facing, at least, academe. Regardless, the present climate is undoubtedly long on questions and short on answers. Figures such as Father Ted brokered hope in times such as the late 1960s and early 1970s. I thus pray my daughters will be served by leaders capable of brokering hope in at least equal measure.

Finally, this book is dedicated to the memory of my grandparents, Harlow and Carolyn Ream and William and Esther Taylor. As the eldest child in my family, I was blessed to spend the most time with them and thus came to appreciate the virtues that defined America's greatest generation. I hope the insights found in these pages serve as a worthy testament to those virtues.

Todd C. Ream
Greentown, Indiana
Advent, 2020

PROLOGUE

A Long Obedience

Being a priest, I guess, means being totally committed to God and totally committed to man and standing between them both, trying to be reasonably close to God, which we never do as well as we should, and being reasonably close to man, which is much easier.

—*Theodore M. Hesburgh, CSC*
From John C. Lungren Jr., Hesburgh of Notre Dame: Priest, Educator, and Public Servant (1987)

People closest to us are often the most difficult to appreciate with the clarity they rightfully deserve. At times, relational proximity blurs our vision. At other times, historical proximity is the culprit. Sentimentality may impair our impressions of individuals with whom we are relationally close while convenient political labels such as "conservative" or "liberal" may impair our impressions of individuals with whom we historically share ties. Regardless, such proximity often impacts our abilities to be as clear-eyed as is otherwise ideal.

Theodore M. Hesburgh, CSC, may be one of those figures for the foreseeable future. As the most recognized priest and university president of the latter half of the twentieth century, many Americans still recognize his name and know something of his legacy. As one draws geographically closer to where Hesburgh expended his greatest personal and professional energies—Notre Dame, Indiana, Washington, DC, and the Vatican—Hesburgh's name is not only immediately recognized but associated with impressions about the value of his life and work that often border on mirroring the polarized nature of the wider culture.

For example, following his death in 2015, Hesburgh was the focus of several personal memoirs and at least one feature-length film. Robert Schmuhl, a noted journalist and American studies scholar who served on the faculty at the University of Notre Dame, published *Fifty Years with Father Hesburgh: On and Off the Record* with the university's press in 2016. A year later, the university's legendary men's basketball coach, Digger Phelps, published *Father Ted Hesburgh: He Coached Me* with Triumph Books. Patrick Creadon, the creator of ESPN's *Catholics vs. Convicts*, released *Hesburgh* at film festivals in 2017 and in theaters nationwide in 2018. While each effort is commendable and worthy of serious consideration, the very nature of those projects makes it difficult for their creators to resist the understandable temptations afforded by proximity.

Perhaps the most widely anticipated assessment of Father Hesburgh's life and legacy came in the form of Father Wilson D. Miscamble's *American Priest: The Ambitious Life and Conflicted Legacy of Notre Dame's Father Ted Hesburgh*. Published by Image Books in 2019, responses to Miscamble's effort proved rather polarized, with some viewing it as sacrilege while others viewed it as sacrosanct. Spirited sessions concerning Miscamble's book in spring 2019 occurred on the Notre Dame campus in South Bend, at the Lumen Christi Institute in Chicago, and at *First Things* in New York, not to mention that the reviews that ran in a number of publications reflected those fault lines.

Like Hesburgh, Miscamble is a member of the Congregation of Holy Cross and serves at the University of Notre Dame. A historian, Miscamble's expertise is in American foreign policy, particularly the Cold War. In addition to a review of both primary and secondary sources, Miscamble's portrait of Hesburgh draws upon a battery of interviews he conducted with Hesburgh at Notre Dame's retreat and research center at Land O'Lakes, Wisconsin, in June 1998. Originally, Miscamble planned to write a "massive 'life and times' biography"[1] for which such interviews would prove beneficial. However, as time passed, Miscamble "began to conceive of a more accessible biographical portrait"[2] which came to fruition in *American Priest*.

That portrait is chronological in nature but divided into roughly two halves—Hesburgh's service to Notre Dame and then to the wider public. Chapter 1 begins with Hesburgh's birth in Syracuse, New York, in 1917, and concludes just shy of his appointment as president of Notre Dame in 1952. Part 1, "Leading Notre Dame," then includes four chapters covering Hesburgh's presidency, ending with his retirement in 1987.

Part 2, "Serving Popes and Presidents," also consists of four chapters, beginning with Hesburgh's appointment to the National Science Board in 1954, but continuing later into his life, as Hesburgh's efforts as a public servant stretched well into the 2000s. Drawing from the title Hesburgh selected for his autobiography, *God, Country, Notre Dame* (Doubleday, 1990), Miscamble's conclusion includes his attempt to come to terms with Hesburgh's legacy.

On one level, Miscamble's work reminds us that Hesburgh was human yet managed to achieve what would exhaust most mortals. Once removed from the realm of the mythological, Hesburgh's achievements then prove worthy of further historical attention regardless of one's assessment of them.

As previously noted, Miscamble's work is less prone to portraying Hesburgh as a mythological figure than other attempts. Hesburgh's autobiography, while an honest appraisal of his life's efforts, leaves readers with the impression that most, if not all, of those efforts came with little strain. The most comprehensive record of Hesburgh's life to date, Michael O'Brien's *Hesburgh: A Biography* (Catholic University of America, 1998), is an impressive catalog of details but also leaves readers with little understanding of the struggles Hesburgh endured as well as the theological convictions that compelled him to persist during those difficult times.

The Hesburgh we encounter in Miscamble's work is someone whose achievements are heroic, and therefore arguably more impressive. In essence, they were achieved by someone who did so despite both failings and frailties. For example, neither Hesburgh nor O'Brien provide readers with the sense of the strain that the student unrest of the 1960s and early 1970s left on Notre Dame's president. However, Miscamble's portrait of Hesburgh not only includes details concerning Hesburgh's efforts to hold the line with students on one side and President Nixon on the other, but also the physical and emotional strain exacted by such efforts.

Hesburgh's impressive record of achievement is also not above criticism, and Miscamble issues at least two. First, in relation to Hesburgh's leadership of Notre Dame, Miscamble raises questions as to whether Hesburgh's pursuit of the university's status as a premier research university came at the expense of a coherent theological framework. Prior to such efforts, neo-Thomism proved to be instrumental to Catholic universities in such a capacity. Miscamble then argues that Hesburgh "failed to keep the challenge of combining natural and eternal truths clearly before him, and without making a major and formal decision, he began to allow what might be called the pursuit of excellence approach to supplant the pursuit of the truth."[3]

Second, Miscamble questioned Hesburgh's record concerning the practice of abortion. Overall, Hesburgh's opposition to abortion was clear, stemming back to when he delivered the Terry Lectures at Yale University in the early 1970s. For the sake of maintaining amicable relations, however, Miscamble contends Hesburgh remained "largely silent" on the matter,[4] especially when working with Democratic politicians such as Jimmy Carter and groups such as the Rockefeller Foundation.

Miscamble's criticisms may challenge mythological perceptions of Hesburgh. Allowing those mythological perceptions to linger, however, would preclude Hesburgh's leadership of Notre Dame and his efforts as a public servant from receiving their full due. The truth of the matter is a human being with failings and frailties served as Notre

Dame's president for thirty-five years while also serving popes and presidents in countless ways. Such efforts are common for mythological figures but rare for humans. Miscamble's work thus begins the process of tilling the ground for a "massive 'life and times' biography."

On another level, however, Miscamble failed to come to terms with what animated Hesburgh, and thus Miscamble's criticisms tend to fall prey to convenient political labels such as "conservative" or "liberal." As a result, perhaps the most miscast of Miscamble's remarks is that Hesburgh "was the accommodating and acceptable priest" who "became caught in the embrace of an increasingly secular liberal establishment."[5] In the end, Miscamble believes Hesburgh "influenced the establishment much less than the technocratic and utilitarian establishment manipulated him."[6]

While arguably not fully wrong, Miscamble's assessment of Hesburgh at this juncture is not fully correct. Despite being a fellow priest, Miscamble spends little time exploring how Hesburgh understood his calling. Doing so demands one go all the way back to Hesburgh's dissertation and first book, *The Theology of Catholic Action*, and then trace how Hesburgh's views of the priesthood, one who mediates between God and humanity, the infinite and the finite, the just and the unjust, influenced how he understood himself. Doing so would demand one explore how Thomas Aquinas's understanding of such a concept, especially as interpreted by Jacques Maritain, impacted Hesburgh. What would then emerge may still merit criticism, but that criticism would transcend categorizations such as liberal or conservative.

One's assessment of Hesburgh would thus still likely note his imperfections. However, that assessment would begin and end with what animated Hesburgh. Criticism thus may prove more penetrating while praise proving more laudatory. To date, perhaps the assessment of Hesburgh that comes the closest to doing so is the very first, John C. Lungren Jr.'s *Hesburgh of Notre Dame: Priest, Educator, Public Servant*. Timed by Sheed and Ward to be released in conjunction with Hesburgh's retirement from the Notre Dame presidency in 1987, Lungren concludes with an extensive quote from Hesburgh:

You [as a priest] have to stand between God and man and all that involves, between sin and goodness, between arrogance and knowledge, between being uncared for and caring, standing in a thousand human situations between God and man, trying to bring the message of God to man and man's petitions to God.[7]

Those thousand situations mean that one called to mediate between God and humanity is defined by a long obedience that may, in fact, lead one in an unfathomable number of directions. As a result, Lungren also quoted Hesburgh as acknowledging, "Being a priest, I guess, means being totally committed to God and totally committed to man and standing between them both, trying to be reasonably close to God, which we never do as well as we should, and being reasonably close to man, which is much easier."[8]

When that "massive 'life and times' biography" of Hesburgh is written, what will first prove to be essential is that its author comes to terms with how Hesburgh understood himself as a priest and as a mediator between God and humanity. The details that then follow can be measured against that understanding and, in turn, how successful Hesburgh was at being "totally committed to God and totally committed to man." Recording the details of Hesburgh's life in such a manner would take a volume many times longer than the one you presently hold. What the book you do hold hopefully offers, however, is an understanding of what animated Hesburgh and thus when such a biography is undertaken, how it might be framed.

INTRODUCTION

"THE MOST FUNDAMENTAL THING I DO"

The priest is a man in the middle and, as a mediator, he bridges the gap between the human and the divine, between time and eternity.

I never wanted to be anything but a priest, which is in itself a great and unearned grace. I hope to live and die a priest, nothing more, but nothing less either.

—Theodore M. Hesburgh, CSC
Commencement Address, Immaculate Conception Seminary, 1983

On February 27, 2015, Father John I. Jenkins, president of the University of Notre Dame, wrote to the university community:

> *Veni Sancte Spiritus.* Come Holy Spirit. With these daily words of prayer, Rev. Theodore M. Hesburgh, C.S.C., implored the Holy Spirit to fill the hearts of the faithful and to kindle in us the fire of God's love. Last night, at the age of 97 and after 71 years of priestly ministry in the Congregation of Holy Cross, Father Ted has gone home to the Lord.[1]

A predecessor of Father Jenkins, Hesburgh's thirty-five-year presidency was the longest in Notre Dame's history. Over the course of that tenure, Hesburgh not only survived the tumultuous events of the late

1

1960s and early 1970s, but he also transformed the academic reputation of the university into one rivaling the excellence of its legendary football program.

As a result, Scott Jaschik, editor of *Inside Higher Ed*, wrote the same day that "Father Hesburgh was a legendary figure not only at Notre Dame, which grew and transformed in significant ways under his leadership, but for American higher education." Jaschik noted that Hesburgh's influence extended far beyond the Notre Dame campus, claiming Hesburgh "was a national figure on issues such as civil rights, serving on numerous federal commissions and speaking out on a range of issues."[2]

Newspapers across the country also ran obituaries noting Hesburgh's legacy. In the *New York Times*, Anthony DePalma referred to Hesburgh as "the former president of the University of Notre Dame who stood up to both the White House and the Vatican as he transformed Catholic higher education in America and raised a powerful moral voice in national affairs."[3]

Nick Anderson of the *Washington Post* saw Hesburgh as "a transformative figure in Catholic higher education who led the University of Notre Dame for 35 years and wielded influence with U.S. presidents on civil rights and other charged issues of his era."[4]

Kate Thayer of the *Chicago Tribune* noted how "Hesburgh carried through on bold ideas that supporters say reshaped a college known mostly for its football team into a prominent academic institution." For his efforts beyond the campus, Hesburgh "was awarded a Presidential Medal of Freedom from President Lyndon Johnson in 1964, and a Congressional Gold Medal in 1999."[5]

Tom Coyne of the *Los Angeles Times* focused on how Hesburgh "helped build Notre Dame into an academic power while championing human rights around the globe, including civil rights and immigration reform and Third World development."[6]

Back at Hesburgh's adopted home, Sarah Mervosh, Megan Doyle, and Ann Marie Jakubowski of Notre Dame's *The Observer* considered their former president "one of the most influential figures in higher education, and whose dedication to social issues brought him worldwide recognition."[7]

Perhaps more than any other American university president or priest, Hesburgh's efforts garnered him the highest forms of recognition bestowed upon civilians. To begin with, Hesburgh was among the class upon whom President Lyndon Johnson conferred the Presidential Medal of Freedom in 1964, with the other five being Lewis Mumford, Helen Keller, Walt Disney, John Steinbeck, and Reinhold Niebuhr. During the presidency of Barack Obama, the Presidential Medal of Freedom was described as "the Nation's highest civilian honor, presented to individuals who have made especially meritorious contributions to the security or national interests of the United States, to world peace, or to cultural or other significant public or private endeavors."[8]

In 1999, Congress announced that President Bill Clinton would confer upon Hesburgh the Congressional Gold Medal for his "outstanding and enduring contributions to American society through his activities in civil rights, higher education, the Catholic Church, the Nation, and the global community."[9] The other recipient Congress chose to recognize that year was Rosa Parks.

In a ceremony held on the University of Notre Dame campus on September 1, 2017, the United States Postal Service unveiled a Forever Stamp bearing an oil painting of Hesburgh completed by Tim O'Brien. Postmaster General and CEO Megan J. Brennan noted that Hesburgh is "considered one of the most important educational, religious and civic leaders of the 20th century." As a result, "The Postal Service is pleased to issue a new Forever Stamp honoring Father Theodore Hesburgh."[10]

Hesburgh's record of achievement also earned him a world record: the most honorary degrees conferred by colleges and universities, a total of 150. Hesburgh received his first honorary degree in 1954 from Le Moyne College in his hometown of Syracuse, New York, and his last from the University of San Diego in 2002.[11]

In the end, these details suggest that Hesburgh was one of the twentieth century's most prominent public intellectuals. Not only that, but he was arguably one of the Church's most prominent examples of a public intellectual. For historical reasons alone, those arguments make Hesburgh's legacy worthy of considerable attention. However, at least two other reasons—one particular to the age in which we live and one particular to people of Christian faith—heighten the need for such attention.

First, the present political climate is polarized, if not downright fragmented. Wading into debates concerning how people are called to live together leaves one susceptible to criticism not only from previously unforeseen sources, but also from sources willing to resort to shrill or even hostile tactics. For example, regardless of whether one thinks that Brett Kavanaugh was worthy of appointment to the Supreme Court in 2018, few would likely argue that the tone of the debate surrounding his appointment was worthy of that concerning a seat on the highest court in the United States. Some would-be public intellectuals are understandably fearful of entering the fray, while others are not above trading shrill theatrics for the substance needed to advance a vison of the common good. As a result, the influence public intellectuals exert is now too often limited to bands of individuals previously disposed to agree with them.

Second, a larger challenge faces the person who believes that Christianity plays a role in these conversations. On one level, the present age is one in which truth is still confirmed by narrow standards of scientific naturalism or modern science. If one cannot immediately access a particular reality through one of the senses, then such a reality must not exist. Theology or the language of faith is still of considerable value, but its sphere of influence is all too often limited to one of personal devotion. What people may believe to be true as a result of the practice of their faith may be true for them. The challenge, however, comes when people seek to exert influence based upon those beliefs beyond what is often perceived to be their private lives.

To find evidence supporting this claim, one needs to look no further than the confirmation hearing now Supreme Court Justice Amy

Coney Barrett experienced when a nominee for the United States Seventh Circuit Court of Appeals. For example, Senator Dianne Feinstein of California told Barrett during her confirmation hearing, "I think in your case, professor, when you read your speeches, the conclusion one draws is that the dogma lives loudly within you, and that's of concern when you come to big issues that large numbers of people have fought for years in this country."[12]

Barrett's presence on the shortlist for a seat on the Supreme Court eventually filled by Brett Kavanaugh also brought up questions of how her faith and, in particular, her involvement in a Catholic lay movement known as People of Praise, might impact her legal decisions.[13] Barrett's faith, however, did not publicly register the same concerns when she was named a nominee for the Supreme Court in 2020. Commentators such as the Associated Press's Mary Clare Jalonick and Elana Schor speculated senators such as Feinstein decided to make Barrett's judicial record and not her faith their primary focus. Their reason for doing so, Jalonick and Schor note, is senators, particularly Democratic senators, were wary of missteps that could hurt their bid to wrest back control of the White House and the Senate majority."[14]

Whether or not one agrees with the views Hesburgh held (and he was often the first to acknowledge he had critics), his example as the Church's public intellectual is not only historically significant but also instructive in the present. As a gift from God, faith is not to be cordoned off in one's private life. In contrast, faith should animate one's whole being and, in turn, expose the distinction between public and private as one of human creation and convenience. Hesburgh's story is not the only one that points us to humanity's created potential. History is replete with accounts of how God's gift of faith enabled individuals to appreciate their potential as beings created in God's own image. Hesburgh's story, however, is instructive for children of modernity who are susceptible to allowing their faith to be socially sequestered to the private sphere of their lives.

THE PROMISE OR PERIL OF THE PUBLIC INTELLECTUAL

In the broadest terms, public intellectuals are "persons who exert a large influence in the contemporary society through their thought, writing, or speaking."[15] Such people often hold appointments in colleges and universities, but that is not always the case. Such people often but not always share their ideas with people living in a particular time and place. What is always the case? Public intellectuals draw upon ideas from their otherwise highly specialized forms of training as resources in addressing questions or challenges influencing some sector of the wider public. Intellectuals, in contrast, may work with the same ideas but do so in ways that are rarely, if ever, shared with the wider public.

Hesburgh's story is instructive not only for people of faith, but also for public intellectuals as a whole. A quick review of books and articles related to intellectuals and their ability to serve the wider public often uncovers titles indicating that something has gone awry. For example, perhaps the most frequently cited of these works, Richard A. Posner's *Public Intellectuals*, bears the subtitle *A Study of Decline*. According to Posner, a former judge who served on the U.S. Seventh Circuit Court of Appeals and is now a professor at the University of Chicago's Law School, part of the problem is "public-intellectual work is becoming less distinctive, less interesting, and less important."[16]

Even though Posner launched that argument in 2001, its relevance has grown since then. In particular, he noted that such work has become "entertainment goods and solidarity goods, as well as information goods."[17] Although the rise of social and other communication media have given wider swaths of people access to platforms on which they can share their ideas, today's public intellectuals must somehow rise above the noise. As a result, they are at times tempted to do so by being noisier than other individuals, clamoring for the attention of some segment of the public.

Posner is not alone in his concerns about the ability of intellectuals to add to or elevate the state of the discussions taking place beyond the walls of academe. In 1987, Russell Jacoby, a historian at UCLA, noted that the scholars who may have generated such work, even if the work they generated was "less distinctive, less interesting, and less important," had succumbed to a larger problem in that they "never appeared." He acknowledged that "a public that read serious books, magazines, and newspapers has dwindled," but the public is not solely to blame. At the core of his argument, Jacoby focused on how "younger intellectuals no longer need or want a larger public; they are almost exclusively professors. Campuses are their homes, colleagues their audience, monographs and specialized journals their media."[18] Their work may be "less distinctive, less interesting, and less important." However, if they view only their academic peers as their audience, do they really care whether their ideas are of interest or accessible to the public?

Although John Michael, an English professor at the University of Rochester, shared Posner's and Jacoby's general concern about the state of public intellectuals, in *Anxious Intellects: Academic Professionals, Public Intellectuals, and Enlightenment Values*, he contended that an even wider array of forces is also to blame. For intellectuals, Michael agrees, "Campuses are their homes, colleagues their audience, monographs and specialized journals their media." He also noted that the decision by scholars to limit the expression of their ideas to their most immediate peers came because of the belief "that the status of intellectuals, an issue fundamental to our work as intellectuals, remains confused."[19]

Michael went on to argue the "fundamentally conflicted situation"[20] of the present state of politics is what facilitates much of this confusion. Although *Anxious Intellects* was published in 2000, one could reasonably argue that those "embattled grounds"[21] have grown more contested over the past two decades. As a result, intellectuals face the choice of staying in the relatively safe harbors of their specialized disciplines or pushing out for seas framed by ever-darkening skies.

Amitai Etzioni, a sociologist who served at George Washington University, was not so quick to point to larger conditions or even to follow Posner's lead that public intellectuals are in decline. In fact, Etzioni contended in the introduction to *Public Intellectuals: An Endangered*

Species? that "(a) [public intellectuals] have far from disappeared, (b) their contact with the governing elites has increased and so, it seems, has their influence." Part of the challenge Etzioni noted is that "(c) while such contact may have weakened criticism from [public intellectuals] who work or want to work with the powers that be, there is no shortage of outsiders who strongly challenge those in power."[22] Thus, public intellectuals may not be in decline, but their voices now compete with others in spaces they once dominated.

In that same volume, Jean Bethke Elshtain, a political philosopher who served at the University of Chicago, argued that when working within such spaces, scholars may also lack the intellectual dexterity needed to be of ongoing relevance to the public. In particular, Elshtain argued, "Because they are generally better at living in their heads than at keeping their feet on the ground, intellectuals are more vulnerable than others to the seductions of power that come with possessing a worldview whose logic promises to explain everything, and perhaps, in some glorious future, control and manage everything."[23]

Just to be clear, the seduction to which intellectuals fall prey may not be access to decision-makers or people in power, but access to ideas that promise more pervasive forms of power than those ideas can rightfully deliver.

As a result, Elshtain contended, "Those who treat every issue as if it fit within the narrative of moral goodness on one side and venality and inequity on the other become so wearying."[24] The ideas that allow an intellectual to be of service to the public in relation to one issue may not prove to be beneficial in relation to the next. As a result, the same structures ethicists may draw upon when assessing, for example, the possibility of a just war between two nations may not serve them well when assessing the possibility of a just war between a nation and a multinational group of militants. In the end, those thought structures may be the same. Regardless, Elshtain's point was that scholars at least need to entertain the question concerning how they define and apply goodness and venality.

In one of his last published essays, Hesburgh asked, "Where Are

College Presidents' Voices on Important Public Issues?" As was widely discussed by that time (2001), Hesburgh noted that scholars and, in particular, college presidents, had abandoned questions plaguing the public. According to Hesburgh, "Once upon a time chief executives in higher education talked to the press about military policy in the same breath as the Constitutional amendment for the 18-year-old vote, but I wonder whether we'd hear them taking stands on similar topics now."[25]

In Hesburgh's assessment, those changes speak to "changes in the culture of higher education and how presidents view their roles as spokespersons on important public issues." On one level, he argued presidents are to blame for abandoning the public and, in turn, exemplifying that abandonment to their colleagues. On another level, he also contended that the size of the universities that many presidents now lead means they are "simply too busy to speak out on issues beyond the immediate concern of their institutions." Such institutions demand their leaders "play an ever-larger role in raising money." In that article, Hesburgh contended, "It is tough enough to maintain an irenic atmosphere on a campus without inviting criticism for taking stands outside the academy that will inevitably alienate one constituency or another."[26] One can reasonably assume those pressures have only grown.

Regardless, Hesburgh believed presidents "are custodians of institutions where independent, ethical, and compassionate thinking must flourish."[27] In partnership with other scholars on campus, the colleges and universities that presidents lead must flourish so they can fulfill their respective missions and also provide their fellow citizens with opportunities to do likewise.

CATHOLICS IN A PROTESTANT AMERICA

To understand the unique role Hesburgh played, one must also come to terms with the discrimination many Catholics faced even in the years shortly after World War II. The presence of Catholics in what became the United States dates to 1565 with what is now Saint Augustine, Florida, being the oldest ongoing settlement. However, the Catholic population that existed in the United States did so with very few clergy and without a bishop. In *The Faithful: A History of Catholics in America*, James M. O'Toole, a historian at Boston College, noted, "In Maryland, according to a report to Rome in 1780, there were almost 16,000 Catholics (including 3,000 slaves) but only nineteen priests; in Pennsylvania, there were 7,000 Catholics and five priests, in New York City, fifteen hundred Catholics and not a single priest."[28] In 1789, John Carroll was appointed the first bishop, the bishop of Baltimore, but at that time the diocese he led included all of what then defined the United States.

Many Catholics faced discrimination at the hands of the Protestant majority at least through Hesburgh's adolescent years. O'Toole noted, "Nativist anti-Catholicism came and went in cycles, roughly parallel to successive waves of immigration between the 1840s and the 1920s."[29] In particular, Catholics were often portrayed as, at best, possessing split loyalties between their new home in the United States and the papacy in Rome.

When Hesburgh was eleven years old, the governor of his home state of New York, Al Smith, became the first Catholic to run as the presidential candidate of a majority political party—in Smith's case, the Democratic Party. In terms of the popular vote, Smith lost 60 percent to 40 percent. In terms of the electoral college, Smith's loss in 1928 appeared even more decisive at 444 to 87. The "campaign had been an ugly one," and Smith's "religion had been the unavoidable issue." As a result, O'Toole contended that the nature of Smith's loss "seemed at the time to foreclose the possibility that a Catholic could ever attain the nation's highest office."[30]

While discrimination against Catholics and the ethnic populations they represented eased over the course of Hesburgh's lifetime, in 1949—just three years before he accepted the presidency of the University of Notre Dame—Paul Blanshard's *American Freedom and Catholic Power* was a bestseller. In that work, Blanshard opened by noting that although Catholics were a religious minority for most of their history in the United States, such was no longer the case. However, the national threat they posed was not merely due to their size but their allegiances. For example, when discussing how the Church resolves disagreements between "Church law"[31] and "American law,"[32] Blanshard claimed that "the hierarchy punishes its people with *religious* penalties for following American law."[33]

In the opening to his review of Blanshard's book that ran in *Catholic World*, Jesuit theologian John Courtney Murray contended,

> Mr. Blanshard has about done it, I think. That is, he has given what is to date the most complete statement of the New Nativisim. In the cold, cultured manner of its utterance it is unlike the ranting, redfaced, midninteenth-century Nativism. Its inspiration is not Protestant bigotry, but the secularist positivism that deplores bigotry, at the same time that it achieves a closure of mind and an edge of antagonism that would be the envy of a Bible-belt circuit rider.[34]

In many ways, Hesburgh and the service he provided were at the forefront of the influence Catholics exerted in the United States.[35]

The Notre Dame community did not escape efforts inspired by prejudice, religious or otherwise. For example, activities initiated by the Ku Klux Klan reached their height in northern Indiana in the early 1900s with rallies, parades, and cross-burnings taking place in several communities. "Local Klansmen in St. Joseph County [the home of South Bend and the University of Notre Dame] were contacted and agreed to host on Saturday, May 17, 1924, a tri-state meeting in South Bend for Klan members and their families from Indiana and neighboring Michigan and Illinois."[36]

On that day, Klan members were met by a number of anti-Klan demonstrators, including students from Notre Dame. Small skirmishes occurred throughout the day and into the evening. "Several students had torn off Klan robes and hoods from persons wearing them, stole bundles of Klan regalia from others, and then returned to campus with their purloined trophies to exhibit them." Fortunately, "none of the numerous clashes occurring during the day and evening in different parts of the city resulted in serious injuries."[37]

To appreciate just how much matters changed over the course of Hesburgh's lifetime, one needs to look no further than the influence, albeit a complicated one, that Catholics wielded during the second half of the twentieth century. Although charges of "popery" were still present in 1960, the fate of John F. Kennedy's bid for the presidency of the United States proved to be far different from that met by Al Smith's. Although Kennedy was recognized to be reluctant to speak of his Catholic faith, what had once seemed impossible was thirty-six years later a reality.[38]

THEODORE M. HESBURGH, CSC

Before wading into the details concerning how Hesburgh served in relation to many of the thorniest issues that emerged during the latter half of the twentieth century, some additional biographical details are needed.[39] As previously noted, Hesburgh, the second of five children, was born in Syracuse, New York, on May 25, 1917 (four days before John F. Kennedy), to Theodore Bernard Hesburgh and Anne Murphy Hesburgh. Hesburgh's father managed a warehouse for Pittsburgh Plate Glass, and his mother was a homemaker. The product of a Catholic education, Hesburgh's calling to the priesthood was influenced by Father Thomas Duffy, who pointed him toward the Congregation of Holy Cross, a religious order founded in Le Mans, France, in 1837, by Blessed Basil Moreau to revitalize the Church in the wake of the revolution. At the age of eighteen, Hesburgh would leave Syracuse for Holy Cross Seminary at the University of Notre Dame.

Within three years of his arrival at Notre Dame, the order selected Hesburgh to go to Rome and study at the Gregorian University—an opportunity made available to candidates for the priesthood who exhibited exceptional potential. In 1940, World War II forced Hesburgh and his American classmates to recross the Atlantic; he then completed his studies by earning a doctorate in sacred theology at the Catholic University of America.

Hesburgh would contend that the high point of his life came on June 24, 1943, in Notre Dame's Church of the Sacred Heart when he was ordained a priest of the Congregation of Holy Cross.[40] Although Hesburgh initially thought he would begin living out that calling by serving as a chaplain on an aircraft carrier in the Pacific, his first assignment was to serve as the chaplain to veterans and their families who came to Notre Dame to receive their education and populated what came to be known as Vetville.

Before his appointment as president of the University of Notre Dame in 1952, Hesburgh would serve in roles such as chair of the theology department and as the university's executive vice president. Although only nine years separated the point of his ordination from his appointment as president, his presidency would span thirty-five years. Over the course of that presidency, "Notre Dame doubled its enrollment, added 40 buildings, grew its endowment from $9 million to $350 million, increased student aid from $20,000 to $40 million, and upped the average faculty salary from $5,400 to $50,800."[41]

In many ways, those achievements alone are of historic proportion, not to mention they also spanned the student protests of the late 1960s and early 1970s. In many ways, however, those details are just the beginning. Hesburgh also made time to invest in conversations concerning topics such as science and technology, civil and human rights, economic development, ecumenical relations, immigration, and foreign relations. Regardless, Hesburgh maintained those commitments were defined by the fact that "the most fundamental thing I do is be a priest."[42]

Coming to terms with how Hesburgh viewed his calling to the priesthood is essential to understanding how he, in turn, viewed his calling to serve as a public intellectual. To Hesburgh, priests and, in their own ways, the laity were called to embody Christ's ongoing presence in the world. Drawing from the words of Saint Thomas Aquinas, Hesburgh contended,

The priest is essentially a mediator because he joins the greatest of all separated entities: the all-holy God and sinful humanity. Christ Our Lord was the perfect and only eternal priest because, by the central Christian fact of the Incarnation, he joins, in His Person, the two extremes: human and divine nature, the natural and the supernatural. Christ is the *fons et origo totius sacerdotii*, the source and origin of all priesthood. What He is in His Person, He accomplishes in His Work. Redemption, like Incarnation, is essentially priestly and mediatorial. All this is summed up in five words: *Habemus Pontificem, Jesum Filium Dei*—We have a Pontiff (a bridge-builder), Jesus the Son of God.[43]

On their own, human beings could not reconcile the divide their sinful nature fostered between themselves and God. Although the sacrifice offered by Christ was the only means worthy of doing so, Christ also called all who follow him to embrace the calling of his disciples to continue that work until he returned. Hesburgh believed he was called to exert a mediating influence in the contemporary society through public service, speaking, and writing.[44]

As a priest of the Congregation of Holy Cross, Hesburgh believed that "the greatest priestly act of mediation is, of course, the Mass." Furthermore, when one stands at the altar and holds his arms wide in supplication, the priest is "embracing the whole world, East and West, North and South, men, women, and children, good and evil, Christian and non-Christian, believers and unbelievers."[45]

Echoing again the words of Thomas Aquinas, Christ as "the Eternal Priest died for all of them and we [priests] show forth his death and his gift for all every time we offer the Mass."[46] At the time of his ordination, Hesburgh committed himself to saying Mass every day. He was able to keep that daily commitment with one exception. While serving as the chaplain to Vetville, he kept vigil with young parents at the hospital as their infant child fought for life.

Introduction

◊ ◊ ◊

What follows, then, is an exploration of how Hesburgh exerted that mediatory influence in relation to challenges—challenges he did not envision when he first accepted his calling—that ranged from science and technology to civil and human rights. As previously noted, that example is historically noteworthy and thus defines part of this book's purpose, but it is also to encourage readers to think through how God may be calling them to exert in their own unique ways a mediating influence whenever and wherever they live.

CHAPTER I

A LIGHTHOUSE AND A CROSSROADS

> To be such a mediator, the Catholic university, as a universal, must have a foot and an interest in both worlds, to understand each, to encompass each in its total community, and to build a bridge of understanding and love.
>
> —*Theodore M. Hesburgh, CSC*
> *University of Notre Dame, 1967*

Among his other contributions to the Church, Saint John Henry Newman's *The Idea of a University* became the most frequently cited appraisal of what defines the university. Since its publication, that work attained a near-canonical standing among leaders of Catholic colleges and universities as well as their secular counterparts. Jacques Barzun, the former provost of Columbia University, referred to Newman as the "greatest theorist of university life."[1]

Yale University Press included *The Idea of a University* as one of the volumes in its Rethinking the Western Tradition series, alongside René Descartes's *Discourse on Method and Meditations on First Philosophy*, Matthew Arnold's *Culture and Anarchy*, and Niccolò Machiavelli's *The Prince*. When introducing Newman's work, Frank M. Turner, Yale's former provost, argued, "In the almost century and a half since its publication, John Henry Newman's *The Idea of a University* has exerted extraordinary influence over the discussion and conceptualization of higher education."[2]

The origins of *The Idea of a University* reside with lectures Newman gave in the 1850s in Dublin after his installation as rector of the newly established Catholic University of Ireland. Newman initially published some of those lectures as pamphlets; in 1873, they were published under one cover, with the title it bears to this day.[3] Since then, efforts to appraise the purpose of the university—and especially the Catholic university—have almost always been offered in the wake of Newman's influence.

As a student, scholar, and teacher of theology, Theodore Hesburgh was well acquainted with Newman's influence by the time he assumed the presidency of the University of Notre Dame in 1952. Hesburgh committed himself to capitalizing on the "timeless principles in Newman's idea" but doing so for "a completely different university in a completely different kind of world."[4] Like Newman, Hesburgh viewed the prime challenge before the university as being the same: "the need for wisdom, not merely the pragmatic prudence of day-to-day decisions, but the age-old Christian wisdom that understands the whole of creation and man's place in this pattern."[5]

Shortly after being installed as president, one of the first individuals Hesburgh consulted in his efforts to comprehend Newman's work was Leo R. Ward, CSC, and Ward's *Blueprint for a Catholic University*.[6] In the preface to Ward's memoir, *My Fifty Years at Notre Dame*, Hesburgh offered, "It was his [Ward's] writing on the Catholic university that, as he rightly observed, particularly interested and influenced me when I, too, returned to Notre Dame to teach and then to help create an ever greater Catholic university here." Despite his affinity for Ward, and Ward's assessment of the university, Hesburgh also noted in that preface that he "found him [Ward], for our present purposes, much more helpful than Cardinal Newman, although he is in the tradition of Newman's *Idea of a University*."[7]

That sense of conviction only expanded over the course of Hesburgh's first decade in office. In the autumn of 1955, John Tracy Ellis published "American Catholics and the Intellectual Life" in *Thought*. Ellis argued, "The weakest aspect of the Church in this country lies in its failure to produce national leaders and to exercise commanding influence in intellectual circles." Ellis went on to contend that "the presence of so widespread a prejudice among the great majority of the population prompts the minority to withdraw into itself and to assume the attitude of defenders of a besieged fortress."[8]

Hesburgh committed himself to addressing those challenges: the challenge before Notre Dame to produce national leaders, command influence in intellectual circles, and "to be a Catholic Princeton."[9] As a result, such aspirations demanded that Hesburgh, at some level, break ranks with Newman, and in 1962 he would write "Looking Back at Newman" for *America*. There, Hesburgh contended that "Newman foresaw trouble, but [he] hardly could have imagined all the trouble that actually occurred."[10]

The trouble Hesburgh referenced included two world wars, the Cold War, and the proliferation of science at a rate that far outpaced the wise use of many of its findings. Although neither a convent nor a seminary, through teaching and learning, Newman's university was "a place to fit men of the world for the world."[11] The university Hesburgh had in mind, a "Catholic Princeton," was defined by the changes he previously noted to teaching, service, and research. The ability to mediate between the matters of heaven and earth defined Hesburgh's Catholic Princeton.

THE MEDIATORY CALLING OF THE CATHOLIC UNIVERSITY

Reflecting that definition, on February 9, 1962, *Time* featured an artistic rendering of Hesburgh on its cover. In his hand was an open book with Mary and the Christ Child on one page and mathematical equations on the opposite. Neither of what those pages represented was wholly separate from the other, but neither were the two wholly distinct. The university and the scholars it resourced were called to navigate the infinite array of ways that relationship existed. To open the cover story, Hesburgh offered, "There is no conflict between science and theology except where there is bad science or bad theology."[12]

The article noted that although the educational quality offered by Catholic colleges and universities was, at best, mediocre, that level of quality was changing, and at the center of such efforts was Hesburgh and the University of Notre Dame. Part of the challenge Catholic colleges and universities faced was financial; they did not have the resources needed for a "Catholic equivalent of Amherst, Oberlin, Reed, or Swarthmore, let alone Harvard, Yale, or Princeton."[13]

Another challenge had to do with the apprehension of truth, wherever such efforts may lead. To some, the use of narrow means left little to no room for questions concerning God and God's ongoing relationship with creation. Scientific naturalism operated on the assumption that whatever was not immediately in one's line of sight must not exist. To others, the apprehension of truth, wherever it may lead, meant a fear of what may be learned about God or God's creation.

In contrast, Hesburgh believed that between and, in many cases, beyond these competing views, science and theology in their highest forms lived in harmony with each other and were complementary means to apprehending truth. Toward the end of that article in *Time*, Hesburgh argued that we live

> in a world where most academic endeavor concerns only natural truth, as much separated from supernatural truth, the divine wisdom of theology, as sinful man was separated from God before the Incarnation. If these extremes are to be united, a work of mediation is needed. We must somehow match secular or state universities in their comprehension of a vast spectrum of natural truths in the arts and sciences, while at the same time we must be in full possession of our own true heritage of theological wisdom.[14]

A work of mediation, a work made possible by the sacrifice of Christ and carried out in their own ways by clergy and the laity, was definitive of Hesburgh's view of the university and public intellectuals who go about their work in the Church's name.

Although the priest committed his life to serving as a mediator between God and humanity through the grace administered by the sacraments, the priest and the layperson played comparable mediatory roles within the university, particularly when it came to teaching, research, and service. Drawing upon the Apostle Paul in Ephesians 4:11–13, Hesburgh contended,

> No one is unimportant in the Church, because all of us have the same basic dignity as members of Christ, partakers of His divine life. All truth, all grace, all power, all dignity in the Church, from Pope to peasant, is from Christ. And because we share His life, we also share his work of redemption, not all in the same measure, but all truly participate if the redemptive work is to be accomplished as he wishes.[15]

As a result, the experimental physicist and the theologian, whether clergy or laypersons, participate in the same calling of mediation—a calling to participate in the work to which Christ called them.

According to Hesburgh, what defines such clergy and laity alike and gives their work a mediatory purpose "is a faith in the word of the living God who made the world and gave it a purpose. It is also a faith in an all-powerful God who takes part in every human event, and yet respects the freedom of every human person."[16] Absent such a faith—the impetus to see the relationship shared by the material and the divine, the sacred and the secular—scholars see only what is immediately before them; the horizon defining their line of sight is capable of tracing only the surface of a particular phenomenon of inquiry. Such a line of sight would not come to scholars who practiced their craft in the manner standard for their disciplines. Even more importantly, Hesburgh contended, "Through the sacraments, this life is nurtured and grows."[17]

Hesburgh noted that the frustrated pessimism often plaguing academe stems from assessments of fate or the inevitable. In contrast, the mediatory calling of the Christian scholar, one defined by faith in what Christ made possible on the cross, stems from assessments of the providential work of God. Hesburgh argued, "Optimism then is indeed the order of the day, no matter what the turn of events, no matter how far we have come, no matter how far we have to go."[18]

In the end, Hesburgh believed the mediatory calling lived out by scholars who were attuned by faith to God's providence, and thus viewed the past, present, and future with hope, contributed to both the Church and state that were worthy and reflective of Christ's sacrifice. However, the benefits that this mediatory calling is poised to offer the Church and state are not unidirectional, flowing from the university to the Church and state; rather, by necessity, they are bidirectional. The Church and the state benefit from the wisdom generated by entities that possess the intellectual dexterity and resources to commit their energies in full-time capacities on an ever-changing array of challenges. The university then finds enlargement of purpose as it applies timeless truths to an array of contemporary challenges.

Hesburgh was fond of referring to the Catholic university as both a lighthouse and a crossroads. After circling the globe to visit as many educational, ecclesial, and civic leaders as possible, Hesburgh concluded in a travel diary, "The university, once an ivory-towered haven, is ever more involved in the concerns of the world at large. If we can bring some measure of intelligence, wisdom, and dedication to all or at least to some of these problems, the University's life will also be enlarged and its cherished position more widely justified."[19]

THEOLOGY AND PHILOSOPHY

To exercise its mediatory role, Hesburgh believed the Catholic university needed to provide ample space for theologians and philosophers to practice their craft while doing so in ways that gave purpose and meaning to scholars in other disciplines. He believed, "the Catholic university cannot fulfill this essential function in our day unless it develops departments of philosophy and theology as competent as its departments of history, physics and mathematics." To do so, the university needed "talented philosophers and theologians, fully skilled in their science, as cherished as other scholars on the faculty, and deeply involved in the full range of university intellectual endeavor."[20]

The modern university, however, was defined by reductive forms of research. As a result, scholars knew a great deal about matters that existed in narrowing veins of knowledge or, as critics often called them, "silos." The theoretical physicist, for example, knew a great deal about theoretical physics and, even more so, subspecialties of theoretical physics. The challenge, according to Hesburgh, emerged when scholars needed access to insights from other disciplines to appreciate the value of their discoveries and make full use of them. For that to happen, "theology and philosophy must effectively play an important role in the intellectual life of a university in our times" as they provide "special ways of knowing, of ultimate importance."[21]

Hesburgh believed academe needed the integral humanism detailed by the twentieth-century French philosopher Jacques Maritain. Hesburgh contended the disciplines would cultivate

> the whole man who is really at home, temporarily in time and eternally in eternity, the man who respects both orders, and neglects neither, the man who has been completely revivified by the grace of Christ, whose faith and hope and charity are able to renew, direct, and revivify the things of time, and to achieve the human good in all its fullness in time while ultimately referring it to the eternal good that awaits beyond.[22]

In many ways, integral humanism was a habit, a refusal to participate in an infinite cycle of intellectual reductionism. That habit, evident in the right practice of theology and philosophy on their own and in conjunction with any number of other disciplines, allows one to participate in the work of mediation.

Theological and philosophical insights repeatedly present the scholar, regardless of discipline, with the understanding that the "work of education is in the world, but never completely of the world." As a result, Hesburgh believed that in the university "we have priests and laymen [working] side by side, we are committed to a higher wisdom while working effectively for all the perfection that is possible in the things of time."[23] The challenge is to live in-between, to mediate between the two, and to draw upon and together the most fruitful insights that both the temporal and eternal worlds have to offer. Only then can philosophy and theology, as well as an ever-expanding array of disciplines, find their rightful place and purpose.

FREEDOM AND THE UNIVERSITY

In Hesburgh's estimation, the mediatory nature of the university was dependent not only on the relationship the disciplines shared, but also on the environment in which scholars practiced those disciplines. That environment was defined by academic freedom. Although the contemporary university defines academic freedom as freedom from external pressures, Hesburgh had a far more nuanced view. Freedom from external pressures, whether exerted by the Church or the state, was certainly part of what he had in mind. Just as important as what scholars were free from was what, in Hesburgh's mind, they were free to pursue.

In other words, did scholars have a clear purpose in mind when practicing the craft of their discipline? Or was that purpose a simplistic pursuit of knowledge for its own sake? As previously echoed, in Hesburgh's estimation, the rightful practice of theology and philosophy was essential for scholars to have a purpose in mind for their work.

That purpose, however, needs the assurance that external pressure would not be exerted and impede the pursuit of truth. For example, during the third year of Hesburgh's tenure as president of Notre Dame, the Church, in the form of Cardinal Alfredo Ottaviani, exerted such pressure. The controversy centered on John Courtney Murray, SJ, and a chapter, originally given as a paper, that was to be published by University of Notre Dame Press in a volume titled *The Catholic Church in World Affairs*.[24] According to Hesburgh, a simplified version of Ottaviani's position "was that error had no rights. If you disagreed with Church doctrine, you had no right to promote your view." Murray's position was that "error is an abstraction and only persons have rights. A person's position, held in good faith, has every right to be heard."[25]

Through Father Christopher O'Toole, the superior general of the Congregation of Holy Cross, Ottaviani ordered Hesburgh to suppress the publication of the volume and Murray's essay in particular. Although this demand was part of a larger effort to silence Murray, Hesburgh also viewed it as an affront to the press and the university.[26] In Hesburgh's estimation, Ottaviani's "letter to O'Toole and O'Toole's to me constituted a frontal assault on academic freedom at Notre Dame."[27]

After consulting with members of the university council, Hesburgh informed O'Toole that he "would not suppress the book." If O'Toole ordered him to do so, he would resign. "There was no way I was going to destroy the freedom and autonomy of the university and, indeed, the university itself, when so many people had devoted their lives to building it."[28] He believed the mediatorial calling of the university was at stake. In an immediate sense, yielding to the pressures Ottaviani exerted would compromise Murray's freedom as a theologian and political theorist. Doing so, however, would also compromise all who published with the press and served at the university.

Eventually, O'Toole struck a compromise between Hesburgh and Ottaviani that allowed for the release of the printed copies. In the end, however, Murray's vindication came during the Second Vatican Council when "he was chosen to draft the Council's article on religious freedom" and concelebrate Mass with Pope Paul VI "in St. Peter's at the end of the Council."[29]

FREEDOM FROM AND FOR THE CHURCH

Nine years later, the relationship between academic freedom and the mediatorial calling of the Catholic university once again came to dominate Hesburgh's attention. In 1963, he was elected president of the International Federation of Catholic Universities (IFCU), an organization he believed "was in shambles. It had no independence, no organization, no treasury or office, not even a decent workable constitution."[30] Despite those challenges, Hesburgh contended during his IFCU presidency that the "most important task was to clarify the nature and purpose of the Catholic university, its relationship to the Church and the state and to its faculty and students."[31]

Doing so did not prove easy, as questions in canon or Church law circulated concerning how one was elected president and, in turn, what powers the president and other elected officers had in guiding the IFCU. At the center of the controversy was Cardinal Giuseppe Pizzardo, who headed the Sacred Congregation of Seminaries and Universities (SCSU) and argued elections held by the IFCU had to be approved by the SCSU. At the heart of Pizzardo's concern was that the IFCU be headed by a leader of a Catholic college or university. Technically, Notre Dame was owned and operated by the Congregation of Holy Cross, thus, in Pizzardo's opinion, made Hesburgh ineligible. Eventually Pope Paul VI resolved this challenge, reinstated Hesburgh and others as rightfully elected officers, and worked with them on a new constitution.

When addressing the IFCU's eighth general conference, Hesburgh implored the crowd gathered at the Catholic University of Lovanium in Kinshasa that their universities were to "be among the best of universities, in the full meaning of the word, and to be Catholic in the full contemporary sweep of the Church's concern for worldwide human development in its ultimate personal, social, cultural, spiritual, and even material dimensions."[32] To do so, the Catholic university needed to be clear about its mission and have the freedom to cultivate scholars who could focus on the concerns of the Church.

In preparation for that meeting in Kinshasa, Hesburgh organized meetings of leaders representing the North American region of the IFCU who focused on "basic questions concerning the role of the Catholic university in the world today." In particular, those leaders believed that "the Catholic university is and has been rapidly evolving and that some distinctive characteristics of this evolving institution should be carefully identified and described."[33] Those distinctive characteristics were identified at meetings held July 20–23, 1967, at a retreat center owned by the University of Notre Dame in Land O' Lakes, Wisconsin.

Although the popular name for their study document came to be the "Land O' Lakes Statement," the official title, "The Idea of the Catholic University," demonstrated an ongoing commitment to honor still-evolving perceptions of Newman's *The Idea of a Catholic University*. To begin, the authors contended, "The Catholic university must be an institution, a community of learners or a community of scholars, in which Catholicism is *perceptibly present and effectively operative*." For Catholicism to be perceptively present and effectively operative, theology and philosophy were deemed "essential to the integrity of a university." However, "to perform its teaching and research functions effectively the Catholic university must have a true autonomy and academic freedom in the face of authority of whatever kind, lay or clerical, external to the academic community itself."[34] Although others disagreed with his conviction, Hesburgh believed the mediatorial calling of the Catholic university and the scholars it resourced was dependent not only on the purpose granted by the Church, but also on the freedom to follow where that purpose may lead.[35]

FREEDOM FROM AND FOR THE STATE

To be free to address the concerns of the Church, the Catholic university also needed to be free from the state. Only when the Catholic university was free from the state could the Catholic university be free to address the needs of the state. The dual nature of that calling concretely emerged for Hesburgh in relation to protests initiated by the Vietnam War in the late 1960s and early 1970s.

On one front, Hesburgh sought to guarantee the rights of members of the university community to protest, with the exception of when "protests were of such a nature that the normal operations of the university were in any way impeded, or if the rights of any member of this community were abrogated, peacefully or nonpeacefully."[36] In what became one of his more widely cited memos, Hesburgh told the Notre Dame community that

> anyone or any group that substitutes force for rational persuasion, be it violent or nonviolent, will be given 15 minutes of meditation to cease and desist. They will be told that they are, by their actions, going counter to the overwhelming conviction of this community as to what is proper here. If they do not within that time period cease and desist, they will be asked for their identity cards. Those who produce these will be suspended from this community as not understanding what this community is. Those who do not have or will not produce identity cards will be assumed not to be members of the community and will be charged with trespassing and disturbing the peace on private property and treated accordingly by the law.[37]

On Tuesday, November 18, 1969, students protesting the presence on campus of recruiters from the Central Intelligence Agency and Dow Chemical tested that policy by lying down in front of the doors to the building in which the interviews were being conducted. As outlined in Hesburgh's memo to the university community, the students were issued a fifteen-minute warning. When they failed to heed that warning, their identity cards were collected. In a front-page story on Thursday, November 20, 1969, Notre Dame's student newspaper, *The*

Observer, reported, "Five Notre Dame students have been expelled and five suspended."[38]

While Hesburgh found the mediatorial calling of the university being threatened by individuals within the community, it was also being threatened by individuals beyond the community. At stake, once again, was the freedom of members of the community to protest. He sought to ensure that calling within the community by setting parameters and, in turn, protected the freedom of some to protest while also protecting the freedom of the university to pursue its normal course of business.

The freedom to protest, even under the terms that Hesburgh outlined in his memo to the university community, was also threatened in spring 1970 when the Nixon administration considered working with governors to dispatch National Guard units to university campuses to maintain order. On May 4, 1970, members of the Ohio National Guard opened fire on protesters at Kent State University, killing four and injuring nine others. Eleven days later, members of the Jackson Police Department and the Mississippi Highway Patrol opened fire on protesters at Jackson State University, killing two and injuring nine.

As a result of what became known as the "15-Minute Rule," the Nixon administration came to view Hesburgh as someone who took a stand against protesters on his campus. Hesburgh's response, however, was to argue that the Nixon administration and governors should not intervene in the affairs of college and university campuses. He sent a letter to Vice President Spiro Agnew in which he argued,

> The best salvation for the university in the face of any crisis is for the university community to save itself, by declaring its own ground rules and basic values and then enforcing them with the widest and deepest form of moral persuasion for the good life of the university, and consequent moral condemnation with academic sanctions for any movement against university life and values—especially violence, vandalism and mob action that are the antitheses of reason,

civility and the open society that respects the rights of each and all.[39]

On one level, Hesburgh believed the presence of troops on college and university campuses would incite more protests and increase the chance for more violence. On another level, the presence of troops on Catholic college and university campuses would compromise their mediatorial calling. The university, if allowed to be free to be itself, possessed the resources to address such crises.

When reflecting years later about those days on the Notre Dame campus, Hesburgh noted, "At the height of the Vietnam crisis, we held together on this campus because thousands of students and faculties celebrated Mass together, at all hours of the day and night, indoors and outdoors."[40] In the mediatorial practice of the Mass, individuals who previously saw little of themselves in one another came to see their common identity in Christ. Whether they supported or were opposed to the Vietnam War, that common identity compelled them to wrestle with what transcended their political views and, in turn, informed those political views.

◊ ◊ ◊

Hesburgh was right in asserting that the twentieth century had come with challenges that Newman did not foresee—challenges that would at least have put the university under considerable strain. Instead of testing what challenges Newman's *Idea* could endure, Hesburgh believed the mediatorial calling of the Catholic university called for it and the scholars it resourced to embrace those challenges. Only then could the Catholic university fully embrace its calling and prepare public intellectuals to serve the needs of the world on behalf of the Church.

CHAPTER 2

AT THE MERCY OF POWER WITHOUT PURPOSE

Science is power, and power needs direction to be meaningful. It is man who is the scientist, and science exists in the world of man. This world has total perspectives and man has a destiny beyond science. Science of itself cannot know God, or the nature of man, cannot establish justice, define morality, constitute culture or write poetry.

—*Theodore M. Hesburgh, CSC*
Sermon Delivered at the Opening of the School Year,
University of Notre Dame, 1957

At 5:29:45 a.m. on July 16, 1945, John Lugo "was flying a naval transport plane at 10,000 feet some 30 miles east of Albuquerque, en route to the West Coast." He saw a tremendous explosion approximately fifty-five miles to the south. When recounting the details of that morning, Lugo offered, "My first impression was, like, the sun was coming up in the south. What a ball of fire! It was so bright it lit up the cockpit of the plane." Confused by what he witnessed, Lugo radioed Albuquerque but received no explanation except "Don't fly south."[1]

Approximately forty-nine miles in that very direction, a group of scientists and military personnel was huddled in bunkers on the desert

31

floor, anxiously awaiting the results of a scientific effort that involved approximately 120,000 people who worked at three sites located in opposite corners of the country. Just before Lugo witnessed the "sun rise" from the south, J. Robert Oppenheimer, the scientific director, witnessed what he knew was the dawn of the nuclear age. The fused sand that their "gadget" left behind was known as the Trinity Site at the time of detonation, Oppenheimer uttered the opening line from John Donne's sonnet bearing that name, "Batter my heart, three-person'd God."

Less than a month later, residents of Hiroshima and Nagasaki, Japan, on August 6 and August 9, 1945, respectively, met the power of the gadget's direct descendants, "Little Boy" and "Fat Man." Historians argue that the impact of these nuclear blasts forced the Japanese to offer an unconditional surrender on August 15, 1945, and thus ended World War II. However, debates will likely continue for generations concerning the necessity of this inflection point in the history of science and technology.

Despite the suffering the Cold War fostered in locales such as Korea, Vietnam, Afghanistan, and Nicaragua, to name only a few, leaders of the superpowers who waged it fortunately opted for picking up the red phone rather than pressing the red button. For better and for worse, however, one way to witness the impact of the Cold War in the United States is through the rise in federal dollars given to colleges and universities for research and development. For example, "In 1940, the Federal Government was supporting research and development in our educational institutions at the annual rate of 15 million dollars." By 1961, that rate had "multiplied sixty times to a rate of 900 million dollars."[2]

Theodore Hesburgh was a critical figure in the debates concerning how that funding was used and, ultimately, to what end the federal government was to invest in science and technology. The Congregation of Holy Cross priest and president of the University of Notre Dame received a call in 1954 from the Eisenhower White House, asking him to serve on the National Science Board. When recalling that request eight years later at the California Institute of Technology (Caltech),

Hesburgh offered, "I replied that I must be the wrong man since all of my education had centered on philosophy and theology. Then I was told that President Eisenhower wanted a philosophical and theological point of view represented on the Science Board. What can one say to that? I joined, and my scientific education began."[3] With that appointment, he launched his service as the Church's public intellectual.

The National Science Board was established by the National Science Foundation (NSF) Act of 1950 and is currently composed of twenty-five members appointed by the president of the United States. Drawn from industry and academe, the board was charged with fulfilling at least two roles.

> First, it establishes the policies of NSF within the framework of applicable national policies set forth by the President and the Congress. In this capacity, the Board identifies issues that are critical to NSF's future, approves NSF's strategic budget directions and the annual budget submission to the Office of Management and Budget, and approves new major programs and awards. The second role of the Board is to serve as an independent body of advisors to both the President and the Congress on policy matters related to science and engineering and education in science and engineering.[4]

As echoed in the account of that 1954 White House conversation, Hesburgh was the only nonscientist on the board and the only clergyperson, leaving him to mediate between the temporal as represented by the natural sciences and the eternal as represented by philosophy and theology.

Hesburgh served on the National Science Board for twelve years. His work with the board was not the only way he contributed to discussions concerning the future of science and technology. In the Caltech address, Hesburgh offered that, because of his service on the National Science Board,

Other assignments followed....The Board of the Midwestern Research Universities Association, working on a new scheme in high energy physics, the Nutrition Foundation Board, the Policy Advisory Board of Argonne National Laboratory, the International Atomic Energy Agency—Atoms for Peace—and the Board of the original Physical Science Study Committee.[5]

Hesburgh accepted at least one other noteworthy appointment pertaining to science and technology: he served as the United States' ambassador to the United Nations Conference on Science and Technology.

As in subsequent chapters, space will not afford an exploration of all the details defining these efforts. Even so, in relation to Hesburgh's identity, details follow concerning (1) how his thought developed over the course of his life and (2) how, in this case, he sought to mediate between the eternal truths of theology and the temporal truths of science.

SCIENCE, THEOLOGY, AND THE UNIFIED NATURE OF TRUTH

As Hesburgh stated in the 1962 *Time* cover story, no conflict ultimately existed between science and theology. The warfare of science with theology in Christendom, echoing the title and focus of Andrew Dickson White's 1896 study, was the result of bad science and bad theology. Human beings are plagued by many limitations. In the case of the relationship shared by science and theology, the nexus of pride and finite intellectual capabilities often yielded particularly troubling results.

In one of his first speeches on this topic, at Notre Dame's sister school, Saint Mary's College, in honor of the opening of its new science building, Hesburgh cautioned that any peace that might come between science and theology could not come at the expense of fostering work and research in isolated, disciplinary silos. Regardless of the challenges that may come, the two must live, as with all the other disciplines, in a proper, unified relationship to each other.

Hesburgh assigned both parties equal measures of blame for "silo-ing." In particular, he claimed, "The scientist himself is often so dazzled by the brilliance of his close-up view of reality that he sometimes forgets to relate the scientific fact with the philosophical or theological meaning that can put the scientific fact into the larger perspective of man, his nature, his life, and his God."[6] He then contended, "The philosopher, the literary man, the theologian are equally at fault, for like the scientist, they, too, have focused themselves almost exclusively upon their own disciplines. Historically they have done in their own ages of pre-eminence what the scientist is doing today."[7] Both parties had access to forms of truth. Both parties, however, needed to embrace the creative tension shared by their disciplines to defy what their pride and finitude may otherwise lead them to believe.

Hesburgh believed that humans, due to those limitations, may never come to appreciate truth in its fullest form this side of eternity. At the same time, the best scenario offered by staying within one's own disciplinary silo was peace brokered by mutual ignorance. As a result, Hesburgh argued,

> Now is the day when we must face the herculean intellectual task of achieving the unity of knowledge that will recognize all that is validly known today, and all of the valid ways of knowing. We have had enough of philosophy without theology, theology without science, science without either philosophy or theology, and each of these without the true humanism of the literary arts.[8]

Two years later, while addressing his own faculty at Notre Dame concerning the relationship shared by theology and science, Hesburgh offered, "I know not where this integration can take place if not in a university—where all knowledge is communicated and extended in its totality and, one might hope, in proper perspective."[9]

Although history offered examples of individuals who embraced this tension, Hesburgh saw few contemporary examples. He saw the need as being as much a matter of the heart as of the mind. The need was for "professors and students, eager to teach and to learn whatever can be known by whatever ways of knowledge."[10]

Appealing to the hearts and minds of scientists and theologians alike was not going to be enough for all who needed to be persuaded to take on the Herculean task he proposed. He thus committed himself to demonstrating why the two needed each other and, in particular, the deficiencies facilitated by a siloed approach to knowledge and truth. In that address at Saint Mary's, Hesburgh challenged fellow theologians and philosophers, "The theologian still lives too much in the world of his own to the consequent sterility of his theology. ... The philosopher has ceased to inspire and be inspired, since he has become so fascinated with the shadow that passes that he misses the reality of the substance that casts that shadow."[11]

If narrow practices of theology and philosophy all too often led to seemingly inconsequential abstractions, the reductive inclination of scientific inquiry posed challenges of its own, often moving in the opposite direction. To Hesburgh, "The scientist who is merely and only a scientist has a deep knowledge of isolated, segmented facts, but little understanding of the broad meaning of all things. He possesses great technical skill in doing things efficiently and effectively but is hard put to explain which things are most worth doing and why." What haunted Hesburgh most profoundly in the nuclear age was the technological ability of scientists to produce results apart from an understanding of what good those results were to serve. He thus argued, "The scientist then becomes a person at the mercy of power without purpose."[12]

This message was not one Hesburgh sought to make only to faculty serving Catholic colleges and universities such as Notre Dame and Saint Mary's, but one he brought to colleagues on various councils and students and faculty members at the world's most prominent technological institutes. For example, when addressing his colleagues at the

Nutrition Board at a luncheon in New York City in 1956, Hesburgh argued, "Science is the tool of man, one of many tools that lead to his total perfection."[13]

Regardless of whether that perfection comes this side of eternity, "Science may indeed destroy man and become his master, if science is not understood for what it really is, not worshipped as a kind of false god, all out of perspective in regard to its true meaning and value in the total life of man."[14] One could then hear the echo of the nuclear age as Hesburgh continued, "All power is meaningless without direction. Worse than that, the magnificent power of science is dangerous, even deadly, if not controlled by human intelligence and integrity and wisdom."[15]

On June 8, 1962, Hesburgh delivered the commencement address at the Massachusetts Institute of Technology (MIT). In that address, Hesburgh argued once again that "science and technology are in themselves neutral, neither good nor bad. Most simply, they represent two great realities: knowledge and power."[16]

The education MIT students received, Hesburgh noted, empowered them with competence "in science and technology" and, in turn, they "possess this knowledge and this power."[17] The choice was theirs in relation to the use or abuse of science and technology, knowledge and power. The difference between use or abuse lay in their ability to "give a moral quality"[18] to what they create, to make the purpose of what they create a determining factor in whether to pursue one line of inquiry over another. Although doing so had the potential to yield specific forms of human liberation, the failure to do so, especially in the nuclear age, is that science and technology could "be perverted in our day, to man's great loss, indeed, possibly his utter destruction."[19] Ironically, the Cuban Missile Crisis, which historians remember as the closest the two nuclear superpowers of the Soviet Union and the United States came to war, would occur only four months after this talk.

In the address delivered at Caltech in 1962, with the Cuban Missile Crisis less than a month in the past, Hesburgh proposed "that we do better [than the Soviets], that our science and technology are more attuned to a higher vision of man."[20] In his estimation, the Communists collapsed all of life into a vision for the technology they developed that did not go beyond what materialism and its offspring could offer. A starting point for the cultivation of a good for science and technology was to wrestle with whether "it is time for scientists and engineers to become philosophers and theologians." By doing so, scientists and engineers "might question the moral impact of their work on the world of man in which they live."[21]

Hesburgh acknowledged "both science and engineering may be a spiritually satisfying experience for the scientist and engineer" but that such an experience on its own was insufficient. On one level, the sense of satisfaction scientists would gain from their work "would be greatly enhanced if the individual scientist and engineer knew that his unique efforts were part of a great human endeavor to reverse the historic inhumanity to man."[22] On another level, Hesburgh contended that asking anything less of scientists was unworthy of the creative calling they embraced. In particular, he noted, "Ask anything less, and you reduce scientists and engineers to the level of automatons, and condemn them to the same state that we bemoan in our adversary [the Soviets]."[23]

In Hesburgh's opinion, the way to cultivate such a purpose, to empower scientists and engineers to see their work as something larger than the production of a set of results, was a liberal arts education. In his address to the trustees of the Nutrition Board in 1956, he argued, "The education that has best reflected our effort to give youth today the heritage of the past, as well as visions for the future is liberal education. If we can establish the place and value of science in liberal education, then perhaps we can gain an insight into the place of science in the world of man."[24]

An education for the future, according to Hesburgh, is not disconnected from the past, but rooted in the best of what previous generations had to offer. Certain disciplinary practices, such as logic, grammar, and rhetoric, historically called the Trivium, demonstrated their value over time as a means to elevate one's use of language. As a result, Hesburgh believed, the value of such practices was not merely in their ability to raise one's awareness of what was valued in the past but also to prepare one to contribute in the future.

Although the Cuban Missile Crisis was still six years in the future at the time Hesburgh gave that address, the Cold War was nonetheless in the background.[25] He argued, "Our young scientists should be liberally as well as scientifically educated, if the scientific leadership of tomorrow is to take account of the total human situation." More to the point, "the basic crisis of our times is ideological, rather than military." A liberal education, as Hesburgh envisioned it, would not only prepare scientists to lead the way in terms of discovery, but also do so in a way that did not lose "those great human values that give us reason for survival."[26]

Over the subsequent years, these same themes—the relationship liberal education should share with the proliferating array of disciplines defining the natural sciences—would continue to resonate with Hesburgh. For example, when speaking at the College of William and Mary's 287th Charter Day Convocation in 1980, he offered an address titled "The Future of Liberal Education." There, he reviewed several defining qualities of that future, including what it meant to be fully human. Such efforts, for example, included teaching students how "to think, clearly, logically, deeply, and widely, about a variety of very important human questions."[27] What he called "how-to-do-it courses," although valuable, do not prepare students to assess the "the sum of our lives or the full meaning of our days."[28]

Hesburgh thought that "a combination of all of these other qualities that alone, I think, can emerge from a liberal education" was critical to the proper practice of science. However, "there is an elusive quality that for want of a better expression" he referenced as "learning to situate oneself." Only when one has had the chance to do so in relation to the wisdom of the past could one learn to strive "for the excellence that so often eludes us; to be able to cope daily with the ambiguities of the human situation."[29] Such an education was desperately needed in the wake, for example, of the nuclear age—an age defined by unforeseen forms of those anxieties.

SCIENCE, THEOLOGY, AND THE NUCLEAR AGE

The anxiety that defined the nuclear age was born in the New Mexico desert on July 16, 1945, and, as previously echoed, the threat defining that anxiety was both scientific and theological. On one level, those threats were external and embodied by the Soviet Union and the satellite states it sponsored. While Hesburgh argued the differences between the West and the East were "not quite as simple as the good guys and the bad guys," he emphasized that the Soviets offered a viewpoint of "the nature and destiny of man [that was] forthright and clear cut." Such a viewpoint created a very different outlook; at Caltech, Hesburgh noted, "In their view, there is no question of a Creator of Divine Providence, no eternal destiny, nothing beyond matter and, therefore, the task of science and technology for them is quite simple: to create an earthly paradise by whatever procedures the state determines, without personal freedom or choice on the part of the scientist or engineer."[30] As a result, the dictates of the state reduce scientists to automatons, and their efforts are reduced to achieve a previously determined technical end.

On another level, Hesburgh was concerned over how the Soviets collapsed all of reality into the material and, in turn, the impact of such a viewpoint on the practice of science and technology. Absent a Creator and an eternal destiny for humanity, nothing was left but to create an earthly paradise and, in the case of the Soviets, do so in the guise of the state. As a result, only individuals best equipped to work with material matters, scientists and engineers, were truly needed. When speaking at MIT, Hesburgh made that point in even clearer terms: "It is not illogical that their educational system, from top to bottom, is rather totally dedicated to the almost exclusive production of scientists and engineers, who are this and little else."[31] In other words, Soviet scientists and engineers were, at best, automatons, while graduates of an institution such as MIT had not only the opportunity but the responsibility to be far more, to appreciate and claim the eternal significance defining their material efforts.

As previously noted, Hesburgh believed humanity's inability to recognize the presence of the eternal in the temporal brought with it a whole host of problems that defied both time and place. However, in the nuclear age and in places such as the United States and the Soviet Union, the stakes were arguably higher. In 1985, Hesburgh argued, "What makes the situation uniquely dangerous and potentially catastrophic today is that both of the contending and contentious superpowers have the potential to utterly destroy each other and the world with them."[32]

Before World War II, humanity possessed weapons that could initiate terror in relatively localized settings. After July 16, 1945, that horror was weaponized in ways that could bring civilization to its knees if not its extinction. By 1985, Hesburgh noted the nuclear weapons possessed by the Soviet Union and the United States were then far greater in number and power, and faster in terms of their delivery. The possibility of a nuclear holocaust was an undeniable reality, threatening all of humanity.

Hesburgh proposed that the United States work with the Soviets in relation to science and technology in general and the nuclear threat particularly if both sides appointed a "broad spectrum" of people to engage in such discussions. He argued that individuals trained in areas such as "business and labor, the professions of law, medicine, religion, and education, the military and political order, too"[33] should represent their countries. If the broad perspective forged by a liberal arts education could not be embodied by a particular individual at that time, perhaps forging such a perspective through a broad representation of individuals was the best possible option.

SCIENCE, THEOLOGY, AND HUMAN LIBERATION

On another level, those threats were also internal and embodied by viewpoints held by U.S. citizens in relation to science and technology. Hesburgh questioned whether those viewpoints, in some respects, were different from those overtly held by the Soviets. In the end, both nations appeared captured by the lure of materialism. For example, at Caltech he asserted, "Much of their [Soviet] science and technology is used for pure military purposes, human talent and brain power dedicated to the means of destroying man." He then immediately asked, "Is our record much better?"[34] Not a pacifist, Hesburgh acknowledged the defense of the nation was a justifiable rationale for military spending. However, he also asked, especially in the nuclear age, how much should the United States spend? Were its spending patterns really any different from the Soviets'?

Hesburgh's critique became more pointed when he addressed the propensity of U.S. citizens to view science and technology as ways to find meaning in any number of material goods. At Caltech, he contended, "To a hungry world, we give the image of stored surpluses, better dog food, more esoteric dishes, how to eat more and still lose weight, how to have more appetite and then alleviate the effects of over-eating, how to stimulate and then sedate." In the end, "Better soap, better deodorants, better beer, better cigarettes, better heating and cooling, better barbiturates, better cars, better chewing gum: these seem to be the ultimate blessings that science and technology have afforded us, the highly visible trappings of our American society, the most widely advertised contributions of science and technology to modern-day America and to the world."[35]

When addressing graduates at MIT, Hesburgh questioned the American propensity to use science and technology to pamper "imagined wants, piling luxury upon luxury, and convenience upon convenience."[36] Even if Americans chose to express their materialism in ways different from the Soviets, they were similarly guilty of viewing science and technology as a means to their materialistic inclinations' ends.

In the Soviet Union, science and technology could serve a larger purpose if the state made such a determination. Individuals were not free to do so. In the United States, however, science and technology could serve a larger purpose if individuals chose to do so. Essentially, what if science and technology were "directed against man's ancient enemies of hunger, disease, illness, and ignorance?"[37] When directed by the right purpose, science and technology could "be dedicated to this great and noble work of human liberation,"[38] not as a means of further material enslavement.

The challenge to U.S. citizens, however, was that the use of science and technology for human liberation was "rarely profitable."[39] Luxuries such as "better beer, better cigarettes" and even "better chewing gum" offered immediate financial rewards. Efforts to address the threats posed by malaria or an insufficient food supply would not. Even if means to address those challenges were found, would those means reap even long-term financial rewards? Regardless, speaking to the graduates of MIT, Hesburgh argued "that there is indeed a higher order of values that makes science and technology meaningful, and that these values reside not in science and technology, but in the person of the scientist or engineer." As a result, "the knowledge and power of science and technology will always be a blessing to mankind; indeed in our day, they may help create a physical situation in which human dignity can finally flower all around the world."[40]

◊ ◊ ◊

Hesburgh's initial commitment came in an arena unfamiliar to him—science and technology. Decades, if not centuries, of "warfare" defined the relationship between many scientists and theologians. However, when the Eisenhower administration called Hesburgh and asked him to serve on the National Science Board two years into his presidency at Notre Dame, Hesburgh believed scientists and theologians could share a different relationship. That relationship, one he believed he was called to mediate, was not new but was established by Christ through the sacrifice he offered on Calvary. As a result, the grace Christ extended to humanity was enough to meet the pressing demands of days so disorienting that they could lead individuals who lived through them to think the sun no longer rose in the east—but the south.

CHAPTER 3

EQUAL AS CHILDREN OF GOD

I really believe that the struggle for racial justice and the creation of legal structures to counter centuries-old prejudice was a priestly work. I found that just by being a priest, I was, through no merit of my own, endowed with great moral authority in the eyes of my colleagues.

—*Theodore M. Hesburgh, CSC*
Untitled Address, 1984

Lawrence Beitler's most famous photograph was the product of being in the wrong place at the wrong time. On the evening of August 7, 1930, Beitler was among a crowd of approximately five thousand gathered on the northeast corner of a local courthouse square. On that corner stood a maple tree with a branch strong enough to support nooses configured to hang two black men, Tom Shipp and Abe Smith. As suspects in a case of murder, robbery, and rape, Shipp and Smith, along with James Cameron, had been arrested earlier that evening.

With the assistance of someone whose identity remains unknown to this day, Cameron was spared the rage of "somewhere between 30 and 75 people [who] stormed the jail." Smith was dragged the short block from his cell to the maple tree from which he was hung. Shipp was hung "from the jail window bars." Several men then "returned to the jail and cut down Shipp's body. They carried it to the Courthouse Square, to the center of the town, to hang beside Smith's." No one recorded the last words of the two men. Some members of the crowd "built a fire under the bodies, but it failed to burn them. Others stabbed and spat at the two dead victims." The local sheriff, Jake Campbell, cut down the bodies about 5:45 a.m., "allowing them to fall with a thump to the ground."[1]

Beitler's photo captures the bodies of Shipp and Smith as they hung against the night sky, both savagely beaten, one with his head hanging straight forward and the other to the right. As ominous as the images of the bodies are those of the seemingly unfazed bystanders in the foreground. A young couple in the left corner, for example, smiled as if they were posing for the camera. One man pointed at the two bodies, as if worried Beitler might fail to capture their image. Regardless, no one in the crowd seemed concerned about Shipp and Smith or about Beitler filming them at the scene of such a heinous crime. Perhaps they knew that "not a single member of the lynch mob [would] ever [be] punished."[2]

Four years later, a young Theodore Hesburgh arrived in South Bend, Indiana, to begin his studies at the University of Notre Dame—a mere ninety-six miles northwest of that courthouse square, well above the Mason-Dixon line in Marion, Indiana. Hesburgh's childhood in Syracuse, New York, never gave him the opportunity to interact with any African Americans.

Reflecting on his life and his experience with race relations, Hesburgh wrote, "I was well into my twenties before I had any significant contact with blacks. That was when I was working on my doctorate in Washington [DC]." When President Eisenhower asked him in 1957 to serve on the newly formed federal Civil Rights Commission, he commented, "I hardly qualified for membership in the NAACP."[3] Regardless, once again Eisenhower asked him if he would serve, and Hesburgh agreed.

Hesburgh served on the Civil Rights Commission from its inception in 1957 until 1972, and as chair from 1967 to 1972. The commission was created by an act of Congress in 1957, but many wondered whether forming a commission versus drafting legislation was an attempt to avoid controversy. Senator Edward Kennedy, for example, later referred to the proliferation of commissions as a congressional "cop-out."[4] The six-member commission had no formal power with the exception of issuing subpoenas, thus compelling testimony detailed in reports that could influence public opinion.[5] Hesburgh noted that the commission was "restricted almost entirely to fact-finding and reporting. We enforce no laws. We have no authority to redress individual grievances, no matter how serious."[6]

Regardless, the six-member commission (three Republicans, two Democrats, and one independent—Hesburgh) got to work and "held public hearings throughout the United States, but, especially in trouble spots."[7] As a result, they held hearings in places such as Montgomery, Alabama, Jackson, Mississippi, and Shreveport, Louisiana, to name a few.

Those early hearings largely focused on voting, especially the efforts of registrars in various counties to prohibit African Americans from even registering. For example, during hearings in Jackson, Mississippi, conducted between February 16 and 20, 1965, Jessie Lee Harris, a field worker for the Student Nonviolent Coordinating Committee offered testimony concerning his efforts to register African Americans to vote in Pike County's McComb, Mississippi. In particular, he noted, "16 bombings took place in McComb, and we really feel the reason for these 16 bombings, was because of our activities in McComb. I spoke at Society Hill, tried to ask them to let us use the church for voter-registration class, and about two days after that the church was bombed." When Hesburgh then asked Harris about the fate of African Americans who participated in the voter-registration classes, Harris said that out of 125 who took the test, "many were afraid to go back by themselves and check [if they passed]." Among those who went back, Harris confirmed that "most of them failed." Hesburgh responded, "Mr. Harris, I appreciate the anguish that you and your fellow workers went through to try to get more people registered in a place—in a county where only 2.1 percent of the negro population is registered."[8]

Testimony such as the exchange between Harris and Hesburgh

made its way into "over a hundred volumes of studies in all areas of concern."[9] Through the nature and volume of exchanges that individuals like Harris experienced with members such as Hesburgh, the reports were designed to influence public opinion and form the basis of the commission's recommendations. In 1984, Hesburgh reported, "Over seventy per cent of our [the commission's] recommendations (almost all highly controversial) were enacted into federal law in the decade of the sixties. The federal civil rights legislation of 1964 [the Civil Rights Act], 1965 [the Voting Rights Act], and 1968 [the Fair Housing Act] changed the face of the nation."[10]

Hesburgh's tenure on the commission and as its chair ended in 1972. Under his leadership, the commission issued report cards on how federal agencies were performing in relation to key civil rights indicators. When those reports began to paint an unflattering picture of Richard Nixon's presidential leadership, Nixon's aides lobbied for Hesburgh's termination. Technically, Nixon sought—and Hesburgh offered—his resignation. However, Hesburgh would later report that he was "fired."[11]

Regardless, Hesburgh contended, "Those fifteen years of service on the Commission were among my most priestly and apostolic."[12] As the Church's public intellectual, Hesburgh found himself mediating between the individuals whom structures of oppression cast as the "least of these" and the individuals responsible for creating those structures. Those structures were originally drawn along racial lines. As Hesburgh's work advanced, he realized that the same mediating impulse called him to focus on how structures of oppression also relegated women and the unborn to being among "the least of these."

DEFINING PREJUDICE

In the foreword for Charles Y. and Ellen Siegelman's edited volume *Prejudice, U.S.A.*, Hesburgh offered details concerning why he, as a priest, one called to mediate between the eternal and the temporal, was called to wrestle with prejudice and equality. According to Hesburgh, "There is perhaps no quality of human life that lends itself more to self-delusion than prejudice." Too often, people think they can define prejudice, recognize it when they see it, and, of course, are free of it themselves. In contrast, Hesburgh argued, "No one really wants to be prejudiced, but almost everyone is prejudiced, and only the honest person will admit it, reluctantly and without pride."[13]

Hesburgh made what some may view as a sweeping claim in relation to prejudice—that the finite condition plaguing humanity compels individuals to make rash judgments or claim they know more than they do. Theologically, Hesburgh argued that "fundamentally, this means passing judgement, normally detrimental or negative, on some one or some group, without sufficient evidence to justify the judgment—hence rash judgment." Prejudice is thus problematic on its own. However, Hesburgh's deeper concern was "what makes prejudice so spiritually dangerous is the rashness and irrationality of all that it brings in its train: fear, suspicion, dislike, disdain, revulsion, hatred— all unfounded, and all leading inevitably and irrationally to discrimination, social disunity, and the denial of human dignity."[14] If one were to follow prejudice where it all too often leads, Hesburgh believed it compromised the image of God—the source of human dignity—present in all human beings. Prejudice is thus "not only faulty, but also inflexible judgment, characterized more by emotion than reason,"[15] paving a path to various vices.

In Hesburgh's estimation, prejudice and the vices it perpetuated took place on two levels. First, prejudice exists on a personal level and influences relationships. In this regard, Hesburgh said, "Prejudice is best described as the poison of personal relations, the most divisive element of our society, the most corrosive element of our human nature, since it goes against our reason and falsifies our judgments of other persons, makes us and others the prey of irrational fears and hostilities."[16] Essentially, prejudice drives us to live out of our fears, see others as threats, and maintain our advantage over them. Prejudice compels us to succumb to simplistic or objectified views of others for the sake of our own comfort.

Prejudice, however, did not exist only on a personal but also on a societal level. According to Hesburgh, prejudice "becomes an integral part of a religion, race, nationality, color, or ultimately, culture. Prejudice in this sense gets passed on to all members of society or culture, in the family, in the neighborhood, in the school, even alas, in the church." Prejudice and the social vices it perpetuates are transmitted among members in a particular group at a particular time and from one group in time to the group poised to succeed it. As a result, Hesburgh claimed, "In a very real sense, to divest ourselves and our future generations from prejudice will require profound cultural change in our attitudes, a change from within."[17]

Toward the end of the draft of his foreword for *Prejudice, U.S.A.,* Hesburgh began to envision how the personal and societal levels of prejudice could be combatted. Although he identified the Church's guilt for perpetuating prejudice, he also saw it as an essential part of the solution. Hesburgh thus called upon the educative capacities of the Church to address this challenge when he noted,

> It all begins with education—preachment if you will, but this is just a beginning. Today, more than ever before, the word must be joined to the act, an act of all religious persons in the local community, working together to end prejudice and the fruits of prejudice. There is no limit to the scope of this collaboration for justice and charity and social unity and peace.[18]

According to Hesburgh, the Church was not only commissioned to be a voice for human relations that defied prejudice and the vices it perpetuated; it was also uniquely organized to do so. The catholic, or universal, nature of the Church transcended the lines—such as race and nationality—along which prejudice was often drawn.

Hesburgh believed the Church at its core was defined by a peculiar anthropology, "one of equal spiritual dignity before God and men, a dignity that must be respected and buttressed by the same love by which God loves us and we Him."[19] That anthropology was defined by at least two components that animated all of Hesburgh's subsequent views concerning civil and human rights and the mediating role he was called to fulfill.

First, such an understanding goes all the way back to the first chapter of Genesis, particularly verses 26–27:

> Then God said: Let us make human beings in our image, after our likeness. Let them have dominion over the fish of the sea, and birds of the air, the tame animals, all the wild animals, and all the creatures that crawl on the earth. God created mankind in his image, in the image of God he created them; male and female he created them.

By Genesis 3, details become available concerning the depravity that would also define human beings. Regardless, human beings were created in God's image, bear God's image, and thus in Hesburgh's estimation, are defined by an anthropology that defied prejudice.

Second, the anthropology Hesburgh noted was defined by relations God shared with human beings and human beings were, in turn, called to share with one another. Hesburgh turned to the words Christ offered in response to a question from a scribe concerning the greatest of all commandments:

> The first is this, "Hear, O Israel! The Lord our God is Lord alone! You shall love the Lord your God with all your heart, with all your soul, with all your mind, and with all your strength." The second is this: "You shall love your neighbor as yourself." There is no other commandment greater than these. (Mark 12:29–31)

Hesburgh claimed that this Christian anthropology compelled him to believe all people "are equal as children of God, Our Father; all human beings have equal dignity and an equal eternal destiny; despite the differences of talent or grace, all deserve our interest, understanding, and help, especially the least brethren."[20] As his career with the Civil Rights Commission progressed, these two components of his Christian anthropology defined in various ways how he served as a mediator between the eternal and the temporal, between the oppressed and their oppressors.

DEFINING EQUALITY

Hesburgh could detail what was theologically at stake when it came to prejudice and how the Church could offer a response rooted in how it understood an individual's value or worth. The mediating role he fulfilled compelled him to form responses to the array of challenges facing society. In his role on the Civil Rights Commission, an initial task involved concretely confronting the presence of equality or inequality.

For example, in one of his earliest addresses on the topic, delivered at a conference on civil rights at the University of Notre Dame, Hesburgh noted that "three great dimensions" defined "this whole problem of civil rights." First, he did not "know of any problem in this country that is more personal to each one of us than this problem of civil rights."[21] By "personal," he meant we all know or should know people of racial backgrounds different from our own. Those relationships, especially if informed by a Christian anthropology, are not ones "about which a person can be detached."[22] This dimension of the problem ultimately comes down to the question of who we see when we encounter other people. Hesburgh argued "that each one of us in our own way, within our own sphere, no matter how small or great it is, do our best to see that this equality of opportunity reigns and is not a figment of our hypocrisy."[23]

Second, Hesburgh noted that an organic dimension defined the challenges facing civil rights in the United States. By organic, Hesburgh meant, "Every American would have an equal opportunity to live in the main stream of the political process, to hold office, to vote, to participate, and be educated to the extent that his energy, ambition, and his talent carry him." In later remarks, Hesburgh would become more specific about what he meant by this form of opportunity. For now, however, his organic understanding of this dimension of the challenges facing civil rights focused more broadly on ensuring that "every American should have the opportunity to work where he could do the most for himself, for his family, for his community, for his country, without artificial bars to such work."[24] Addressing those organic dimensions meant using the law in whatever way possible as a means to remove those bars, to allow individuals to be defined by aspirations and talents.

Finally, Hesburgh argued that "the third dimension of this problem is that it is not a responsibility of only one part of government."[25] In order to distribute responsibilities in a way that provided for accountability, the U.S. Constitution was defined by a separation of powers among the executive, legislative, and judicial branches. In Hesburgh's estimation, part of the challenge the nation faced was that one branch, the judiciary, "has been overloaded with the burden of this problem." He contended, "Insofar as it must be solved on a governmental level, it is, of course, going to need the attention of all of the powers of government." Hesburgh was not suggesting that the powers of government were the only ones needed when addressing challenges to civil rights. As previously noted, personal and organic dimensions required attention. He felt the judiciary needed to persist in rightfully interpreting the law, but the judiciary could not "clear up this problem if the other two branches of government go quietly along helping those who openly defy the law of the land."[26]

Hesburgh focused on related themes when he addressed the Illinois Rally for Civil Rights at Chicago's Soldier Field on June 21, 1964, shortly before the passage of the Civil Rights Act on July 2, 1964. He had reportedly received a call in his office that day and was asked if, as a member of the Civil Rights Commission, he would represent the interests of both the Church and the state at the rally. Hesburgh's response? He drove ninety miles from South Bend to Chicago and joined an estimated crowd of 57,000 to 75,000 people. A photo captured Hesburgh linking arms with the Rev. Edgar Chandler, the Rev. Martin Luther King Jr., and Msgr. Robert J. Hagarty while singing "We Shall Overcome." Hesburgh was unaware of that photo by a still-unknown photographer until he was presented with a copy at Emory University in 1988. In 2007, Hesburgh was honored at the National Portrait Gallery when that photo was accepted into the gallery's collection.

In his Chicago address, Hesburgh offered two suggestions rooted in the Christian anthropology that anchored his views concerning the significance of civil and eventually human rights. His first suggestion, directed at both whites and blacks, was that "all we cherish at the base of the great dream of America today demands a dedication to the dignity of man, the God-given dignity of every human being." The result of that dream is that "every human being be given equal opportunity to develop all those human qualities bound up in the wonderful expression of enjoying equal rights to life, liberty, and the pursuit of happiness."[27] He also noted, "Our best and ultimate goal, heaven, is unsegregated."[28]

His second suggestion was directed toward African Americans. As a member of the Civil Rights Commission, Hesburgh stated that "equal opportunity [was] coming more and more—even in citadels of great resistance." He also noted that increasing equal opportunity was "meaningless unless Negro Americans used these new opportunities with great persistence and effort and pride....Human dignity is yours, God gave it to you." As a result, he wanted them to "be proud to be a Negro in this hour of decision. Ask for nothing that you have not deserved. Accept nothing that you have not earned. Demand respect most of all by being worthy of respect, because you have done everything possible to be a good human being." In the end, he believed African Americans had the potential not only to be "as good as White

Americans, but better." He thus concluded by contending "we [white Americans] can learn from you."[29]

If Hesburgh's address to the crowd gathered at Soldier Field was among his most impassioned arguments for civil rights, his address to the American Academy of Arts and Sciences five months later in Boston was one of his most detailed. At the beginning of "The Moral Dimensions of the Civil Rights," Hesburgh laid out his understanding of Christian anthropology. In particular, he argued that humans are endowed with an "inherent dignity and destiny that make a denial of these rights not merely a bad political, economic, or social situation, but a devastating spectacle of the inhumanity of man to man."[30]

Integrating the physical and metaphysical claims about what it means to be human, Hesburgh then noted, "A person lives in self-possession, a master of himself, capable of containing himself, thanks to intellect and freedom." His justification for such a claim was that the "same tradition sees in God the infinite essence of personality, since the very existence of God consists in the infinite and absolute superexistence of knowledge and love."[31]

Unpacking that claim, Hesburgh returned to the work of Jacques Maritain. In particular, when quoting at length from *Principles of a Humanistic Philosophy*, Hesburgh referred to Maritain's argument that humanity "has a spiritual super-existence through knowledge and love, he is, in a way, a universe in himself, a microcosm, in which the great universe in its entirety can be encompassed through knowledge; and through love, he can give himself completely to beings who are to him, as it were, other selves, a relation for which no equivalent can be found in the physical world."[32]

As Maritain echoed and Hesburgh stressed, the spiritual super-existence defining individuals was inherently a God-given form of sovereignty no other person could compromise. At the same time, Hesburgh via Maritain wanted to emphasize that one person's well-being was inherently linked to that of all others. As a result, "If you treat a man as a man ... then to that extent you make effective in yourself his equality or unity in nature with yourself."[33]

Hesburgh then quickly argued that this understanding of equality, and the anthropological understanding that defined it, had at least four immediate implications for how Americans should order their lives. First, this understanding of equality meant "the right to life." To support the need of such a claim, Hesburgh referenced the Civil Rights Commission hearings conducted in Jackson, Mississippi, and the testimony of people from McComb. In particular, he offered that in that one city, with a population of 10,401, "there have been 35 bombings, burnings, and beatings this year without punishment, even of the parties who admitted guilt."[34] As a result, the right to life was the most basic expression of equality and the foundation upon which others rested.

Second, Hesburgh argued, "Another large area of opportunity that remains to be opened to minorities is housing." Through hearings the commission conducted, Hesburgh and his colleagues confirmed "bankers, builders, and realtors, often aided and abetted by public federal financing, close the normal housing market to Negroes and minorities." Based on the understanding of equality Hesburgh derived from Christian anthropology, "the moral imperative is clear. Every American should have equal opportunity to buy a decent home in a wholesome neighborhood, wherever his heart desires and his means permit."[35]

Third, Hesburgh believed all people deserved fair treatment in the "administration of justice, equality before the law." In particular, he asked audience members gathered in Boston on that day to think of their "chances for justice in a county where no member of your race is on the police force, or among the jail personnel, or on the judge's bench, or in the jury box." Hesburgh contended that Americans needed to "tighten the blindfold on the figure of Justice so that justice is indeed color blind and all men are equal before the law."[36]

Finally, Hesburgh's Christian anthropology led him to an understanding of equality that considered "the matter of equal access to public accommodations." He found it unacceptable that African Americans could "travel and not know whether [they] would be able to find a place to wash or eat or rest or sleep, despite the fact that [they] were surrounded by facilities apparently opened to the public." Not affording African

Americans access to such accommodations, in Hesburgh's view, was an expression of "our [white Americans'] own moral blindness."[37]

CIVIL AND HUMAN RIGHTS

As noted earlier, Congress could and eventually did pass laws designed to ensure these expressions of equality for African Americans and other minorities. In some ways, those laws could address the exercise of prejudice on a societal level. As previously noted, Hesburgh also knew prejudice; the deprivation of equality was exercised on a personal level. As a result, Hesburgh argued, "No man is an island in this total sea of inequality. When one man is denied equality, none of us is really free."[38] Equality demanded that changes take place on both a societal and personal level that would thus make the age in which he lived "one of the most revolutionary of all ages of mankind."[39]

That age Hesburgh envisioned—one rooted in his metaphysical claims about what it means to be human and the physical claims about how humans were to live out those claims—led him to recognize the connections between civil rights and human rights. For example, when testifying before the United States House of Representatives Subcommittee on International Organizations and Movements on October 11, 1973, Hesburgh contended that Congress "could broaden the jurisdiction of the Commission on Civil Rights to make it clear that it is empowered to study and report on all of the aspects of the human condition that have been labeled 'human rights' on the international level. This would allow our domestic focus to coincide with our international obligations."[40]

Civil and human rights were rooted in the same metaphysical claims and thus one entity could define their physical claims for equality.

In a speech that would come to define the approach of his administration in relation to human rights—delivered at the University of Notre Dame's commencement, May 21, 1977—President Jimmy Carter sought to "connect our actions overseas with our essential character as a nation."[41] He opened by acknowledging, "Father Hesburgh has spoken more consistently and effectively in support of the rights of human beings than any American I know"[42] and then quickly offered a "foreign policy that the American people both support—and understand."[43] In the end, Carter argued that "Our [American] policy must reflect a belief that the world can hope for more than simple survival—and our belief that dignity and freedom are fundamental spiritual requirements."[44]

In Hesburgh's estimation, the relationship shared by civil and human rights was found in the extension of equality to at least two groups. First, as the 1970s progressed, Hesburgh noted that "a few of the critical pieces of unfinished civil rights business"[45] existed and that "the growing national concern about sex discrimination"[46] was one of them. In a speech before the American Council on Education in 1973, Hesburgh said, "Only last year sex was made one of the additional concerns of the U.S. Commission on Civil Rights, in addition to race, religion, color, and national origin."[47] In January 1976, *Ms.* magazine ran an article titled "Guess Who's for the ERA?" Under a picture of him in his customary Roman collar, Hesburgh was quoted as arguing he was "very much for the Equal Rights Amendment and would like to see it passed in the Bicentennial year as part of the fulfillment of the promise of this nation."[48]

In a more expansive and systematic treatment of women's rights as human rights, Hesburgh pointed to the connection shared by Genesis 1:27 and the U.S. Constitution. "It says that only in being men *and* women is mankind reflective of the image of God. No confusion here, such as 'all men are created equal.'" He then contended, "The best reason for human dignity and equality [is] together they reflect the image of God." When beginning to unpack the ramifications of those metaphysical claims on the physical nature of reality, Hesburgh turned once again to Jacques Maritain and Maritain's claim that "mankind's history is a long uphill growth in moral discernment." In Hesburgh's estimation, "Certainly, the women's movement moves us in that direction."[49]

Second, one of the most pointed forms of criticism Hesburgh received involved his perceived unwillingness to consistently condemn abortion as contrary to Catholic moral teaching.[50] Space does not allow for an exploration of the merits of such criticism. However, Hesburgh contended on several occasions that human rights, including the right to life, should extend to the unborn. For example, when delivering the Terry Lectures at Yale University shortly after the Supreme Court handed down its *Roe v. Wade* decision, Hesburgh said he "must also speak for those who have no voice at all, the unborn children who are so cavalierly deprived of the most basic right of all, the right to life, without which all other human rights are meaningless."[51] Reportedly, those views "prompted a negative response from some of the female members of his audience" who "began hissing at their Terry Lecturer."[52]

In the *Ms.* magazine article concerning Hesburgh's views of the Equal Rights Amendment (ERA), he acknowledged, "When people hear I'm for the ERA, they think right away I'm for abortion. A lot of people read this into it. A lot of people separate the two, as they should be, and I have no difficulty supporting the ERA [and the rights of the unborn]."[53] In one of his most detailed and systematic explorations of the topic, an address titled "Pro Life from the Social Justice Perspective," Hesburgh began by arguing, "One cannot ground human rights, philosophically or theologically, anywhere but in the human person."[54] He continued, "To deny the fetus life, is to deny a human being the opportunity that we all have had to live and love, to achieve a measure of human perfection, to have faith, to experience grace, to consciously love God and aspire to eternal life." In Hesburgh's opinion, abortion thus denies "that for which social justice yearns and strives—full human development and fulfillment."[55]

◊ ◊ ◊

The lynching of Tom Shipp and Abe Smith on the northeast corner of the courthouse square of Marion, Indiana, on August 7, 1930, is but one incident in a long sequence of such events haunting the American conscience. What occurred on that evening was most obviously a physical deprivation of the equality Shipp and Smith otherwise rightfully deserved. Hesburgh would likely argue that such horrific behavior was set in motion because members of the mob that came for Shipp, Smith, and Cameron failed to recognize the men metaphysically as people created in God's image—as people worthy of being loved as one's neighbor as expressed by equality before the law.

The depravity Beitler captured on that night is tragically palpable to individuals who view his photograph years later. Foremost, the treatment Shipp and Smith endured was horrific. The inability of anyone to mediate between metaphysical and physical claims on that night, however, also "left jagged scars down to the twenty-first century."[56]

CHAPTER 4

A GREAT COMMON ENDEAVOR

Ecumenical also and importantly means sincerely standing for something and then reaching out in friendship and understanding to someone who sincerely stands for something different.
—*Theodore M. Hesburgh, CSC*
"Untitled Address," 1985

Angelo Giuseppe Roncalli's brief tenure as pope (October 28, 1958–June 3, 1963) signaled the dawn of a new era for the Church. With John (XXIII), Roncalli selected a name none of his predecessors had selected since the fifteenth century. He then initiated reforms "in Vatican protocol that suggested he wanted a somewhat less formal atmosphere to prevail."[1] Few, if any, saw those departures from the norms of his predecessors as indicative of his signature achievement: convening the Second Vatican Council.

Announced on January 25, 1959, Vatican II also proved different from most of the previous ecumenical councils, which were convened to refute theological errors. However, John W. O'Malley, a Jesuit priest and professor at Georgetown University, noted that John XXIII "intended the council as an invitation to spiritual renewal for the church and for the world."[2] After the completion of efforts made by the Ante-Preparatory and Preparatory Commissions, the council opened on October 11, 1962. The number of participants varied, "but generally there were about 2,400 council fathers participating at any given time," making it the Church's largest council and arguably the largest meeting of any kind in history. By the time Vatican II closed on December 8, 1965, the council generated "thirty-two volumes, many of which run to more than 900 pages."[3]

John XXIII's death in 1963 kept him from witnessing the outcomes of the council he convened. As a result of the leadership of Giovanni Battista Montini, or Paul VI, John XXIII's dream of a second Pentecost continued. In fact, Paul VI's English biographer, Peter Hebblethwaite, even argued Paul VI had "a richer and deeper personality" than John XXIII, "had more worldly contacts, and because of his pontificate—fifteen years compared with four and a half—was of more decisive importance for the long-term future of the Church."[4] The forms of spiritual renewal the council initiated are found in its four constitutions: "On the Sacred Liturgy (*Sacrosanctum Concilium*); On the Church (*Lumen Gentium*); On Divine Revelation (*Verbum Dei*); and On the Church in the Modern World (*Gaudium et Spes*)."[5] Of the four, *Gaudium et Spes* resonated most with Father Hesburgh. In his own dissertation, Hesburgh advocated for a greater role for the laity. In *Gaudium et Spes*, the Church taught the following:

> Let the layman not imagine that his pastors are always such experts, that to every problem which arises, however complicated, they [clergy] can readily give him a concrete solution, or even that such is their mission. Rather, enlightened by Christian wisdom and giving close attention to the teaching authority of the Church, let the layman take on his own distinctive role. (no. 17)

As Hesburgh noted in his dissertation, the twentieth century witnessed several pontiffs and several movements within the Church lobbied for a greater role for the laity. Under Paul VI's leadership and John XXIII's inspiration, *Gaudium et Spes* formally conferred that role.

In addition, *Gaudium et Spes* was part of the groundwork Vatican II laid for greater ecumenical relations, or relations between Catholics and non-Catholics who professed faith in Christ. In 1054, the Christian community was split in two between Catholics and the Orthodox. Five hundred years later, the Christian community would split into several other churches during the Protestant Reformation. Unlike the councils that preceded it, Vatican II invited the presence of non-Catholic observers who were hosted by the Secretariat for Promoting Christian Unity (SPCU).

According to Edward Idris Cassidy, an Australian cardinal and president emeritus of the Pontifical Council for Promoting Christian Unity, "There were 38 observers and SPCU guests at the opening session of the council, and three others—including the two Russian Orthodox observers—arrived in the following days. The observers had a privileged place within the aula [Saint Peter's Basilica] and mixed freely with the council fathers in the coffee bars."[6]

Unitatis Redintegratio, the Decree on Ecumenicism, offered the most pointed details concerning the Church's intention to make Christian unity a primary concern of the council. Non-Catholic Christians were referred to as brothers and sisters in the faith and, despite the present imperfections of those relationships, have a partial share in communion with the Catholic Church. The conclusion of chapter 2, "The Community of Mankind," of *Gaudium et Spes* reads, "This solidarity must be constantly increased until the day on which it will be brought to perfection. Then, saved by grace, men will offer flawless glory to God as a family beloved of God and of Christ their Brother" (no. 28).

When addressing the fall meeting of the Chief Executives Forum in Phoenix in 1968, Hesburgh argued, "This ecumenical movement is stronger today, and moving forward more rapidly than most of us perceive, especially among the young who are generally impatient with what has divided men, more ready to move onward toward those spiritual elements that bring men everywhere together in a great common endeavor that is at once human and divine."[7] As the Church's public intellectual, Hesburgh viewed his mediating role in relation to ecumenism as identifying and practicing those spiritual elements that brought people together.

In eternity, humanity would be capable of appreciating the fullness of God. This side of eternity, humanity needed to do what it could to overcome the moral and intellectual finitude that otherwise defined it and thus participate in that common endeavor, one that was both human and divine. For Hesburgh, that endeavor could not fulfill its purpose if it confused unity for uniformity. He noted when giving the Terry Lectures, "Nothing good that has developed to enrich faith and prayer and community life need be lost as long as we grow together in the unity of our faith, hope, and love."[8]

BETWEEN JERUSALEM AND BETHLEHEM

Hesburgh's most formal investment in ecumenical relations began in 1964, when he received a letter from Amleto Cardinal Cicognani, the Vatican's secretary of state. Paul VI wanted to see Hesburgh, a prior acquaintance; as Cardinal Montini, he had given the commencement sermon at Notre Dame in 1960. In Hesburgh's 1989 address at Vanderbilt University's historically Methodist divinity school, he cited three points made by Paul VI: "My greatest experience during Vatican II—which was winding down—has been the opportunity, after all these years, to become friends with the many Protestant Observers. They are not only great theologians, but very holy men. What a shame that after the Council this great association of Protestant and Catholic theologians, discussing theology together daily, will be lost." Paul VI then had noted, "All my life I have dreamed of a place where this could happen and bring us into eventual unity—not uniformity of liturgical practice, but unity of faith."[9]

Second, Paul VI had indicated that he saw Rome, Geneva, Canterbury, and Constantinople as homes for dialogue. Alas, all of them were too closely associated with a particular Christian tradition. But after meeting Patriarch Athenagoras in Jerusalem in 1963—the first such meeting in a thousand years—he believed that Jerusalem was the perfect place for such dialogue. In fact, Paul VI believed, "It was the only place it could happen, where it all began, where Jesus lived and died and rose again."[10]

Finally, Paul VI, knowing Hesburgh was about to meet with the Council of the International Federation of Catholic Universities, had asked him, "Could you persuade them to create such an institute in Jerusalem for Protestants, Anglicans, Orthodox, and Catholic theologians to live and study together, to work for the eventual unity of Christendom?"[11]

As Hesburgh related the story at Vanderbilt, by this time, he had almost a standard reply to such questions from powerful officials, in this case something like, "Holy Father…I've been involved in many endeavors but ecumenism is not one of them, except in my personal life and actions." Perhaps because this request came from the pope and not a U.S. president, Hesburgh more quickly offered to help. "I'll gladly talk to our Council members about your dream. If we can study the proposal, I'll then let you know what seems possible."[12]

The decision was eventually made "that the project, from the beginning, should be planned and executed by an ecumenical council of about thirty theologians from the main churches and countries of the Christian world."[13] Such a decision stood in contrast to Paul VI's original suggestion, to launch a Catholic center to which others were welcomed. In the end, however, Hesburgh noted that Paul VI "agreed that our scheme was the only unique and workable one."[14]

After two years spent negotiating the details of the purchase of "a splendid site called Tantur between Jerusalem and Bethlehem"[15] from the Knights of Malta (a lay religious order recognized in 1113 by Pope Paschal II[16]), on the day the Jordanian government gave permission to begin construction, "Tantur was captured by the Israeli Army." Only after agreeing that "we would build the Ecumenical Center as an international, universitarian, non-political entity,"[17] did the Israeli government give permission to begin construction.

Beyond the time and energy spent seeking approval from a second government to begin construction, the Six-Day War, as it came to be known, doubled the cost of construction materials. I. A. O'Shaughnessy, a Catholic businessman and Notre Dame benefactor from Minnesota, had agreed to cover the original construction costs; Hesburgh noted that "with typical generosity,"[18] O'Shaughnessy agreed to the revised budget. In the homily at O'Shaughnessy's funeral Mass in 1973, Hesburgh recounted that when faced with a bill for two million dollars instead of one million, O'Shaughnessy had responded, "It's a great and good idea; let's do it and do it now."[19]

The Tantur Ecumenical Institute opened in 1970 with, according to Hesburgh,

> fifty double rooms with balconies, a dozen apartments for families, a library with 350,000 books we brought from our Holy Cross Rome Seminary, and room for twice that number, a large conference room, seminar rooms, kitchen and dining rooms, a beautiful ecumenical chapel, [and] quarters for monks from Monserrat, Spain, who would be our librarians and guest masters.[20]

With O'Shaughnessy, Notre Dame covered the construction costs and assumed Tantur's operating expenses. The Vatican bought the thirty-acre tract of land and leased it back to Notre Dame "for fifty years at a dollar a year."[21] When celebrating Tantur's fortieth anniversary, Hesburgh offered, "I thank the Good Lord and His Dear Mother for their inspiration and aid in accomplishing this contribution to ecumenism, which some might have called a wild dream."[22]

MAKING SENSE OF MARTIN LUTHER

Beneath Hesburgh's most formal investment in ecumenical relations as embodied in Tantur is a host of ideas that fueled such an investment. One way to begin such a discussion is to explore how he understood the best-known Protestant Reformer, Martin Luther. *God and the World of Man*, Hesburgh's second book, originally published in 1950, was a theology textbook designed for use in undergraduate classes at Notre Dame. Here, Hesburgh referenced Luther in several places and did so as a perpetuator of theological error.

For example, when discussing original sin, Hesburgh argued, "This then, is the mystery of original sin: the mystery of our oneness in Adam, a oneness that in the original plan of God should have resulted in our sharing of his marvelous elevation to preternatural and supernatural gifts." He then claimed that "instead of being this, it has become a mystery of iniquity, a sharing of sin and the results of sin."[23] As a result, Hesburgh asked, "Who is immediately responsible for the infection of original sin?"[24] His initial response was Luther and fellow Reformer John Calvin. Hesburgh then summarized this point a few pages later, "The so-called Reformation heralded an actual deformation of human nature, due to the basic theological error of Luther and Calvin regarding the early history of mankind." Hesburgh then contended, "Perhaps the simplest way to approach this erroneous trend is to consider its origin in Luther."[25]

Space does not allow for a full exploration of Luther's view on the matter of original sin and the possible veracity of Hesburgh's claim. However, Hesburgh delivered a lecture at Valparaiso University in 1967, two years after the close of Vatican II and while he was invested in the construction of the Tantur Ecumenical Institute. Titled "The Historical Evolution of the Catholic View of Luther," it points to a change in his approach to Luther. Hesburgh opened his lecture by noting,

> The present Catholic attitude [toward Luther] in this ecumenical age is well expressed by Father Yves Congar [a prominent theologian and contributor to Vatican II], "I know that nothing really worthwhile will be achieved with regard to Protestantism as long as we take no steps truly to understand Luther, and to do him historical justice, instead of simply condemning him."[26]

Hesburgh then contended that "there has been in the past fifty years or so a sincere and conscientious effort on the part of Catholic scholars truly to understand Martin Luther and to do him historic justice."[27]

After giving a detailed exploration of those sincere and conscientious efforts, he concluded "that the Catholic attitude on Luther is [not] anywhere near as favorable in the English and French-speaking world as it has become among scholars in Germany." The difference between the two, in his estimation, was "in Germany ecumenism was really given a monumental push by Nazism which persecuted Catholics and Lutherans alike." He ended with a benedictory note: "Let us hope and pray that this present reformation will unite us as we face together the great modern challenges to Christianity."[28]

ECUMENISM AS AN ACT OF MEDIATION

Even before Vatican II and the emphasis the council placed on ecumenism, one could argue Hesburgh was already developing an understanding of his vocation as a mediator between the various Christian traditions and even between those traditions and the secular world. For example, when addressing the Annual Convention of the National Catholic Educational Association in Atlantic City, New Jersey, in 1961, Hesburgh opened his address, "Catholic Higher Education in Twentieth Century America," by reaching back to the Church fathers and tracing forward the great contributions the Church had made to learning and, as it emerged, higher learning.

Hesburgh argued that "whatever the value of the ages of Catholic higher learning, there is only one age whose value we can in any way measure influence: our own."[29] Despite the wealth of theological wisdom Saint Thomas Aquinas and his contemporaries afforded the Church, Hesburgh contended, "It is futile comfort for a Catholic university in the second half of the Twentieth Century in the United States of America to point with pride to the lively intellectuality and critical vitality of the Catholic University of Paris in the medieval France."[30]

Part of the rationale for his own argument was that the Catholic university existed in "an age crying for the light and guidance of Christian wisdom." Wisdom may be timeless, but the realities in which it must be applied vary across time. For example, Hesburgh noted, "We live today in the threatening shadow of cosmic thermonuclear destruction and theologize about the morality of war as though the spear had not been superseded by the ICBM." No more central task existed, Hesburgh believed, for "Catholic higher learning than the exalted work of mediation in our times."[31]

As previously noted, theology and philosophy played critical roles in the exercise of that calling. However, Hesburgh believed any discipline also had a role to play. In the end, what was needed was "some institution[al] attempt to bring together in more fruitful unity the separated and often antagonistic elements of this pluralistic society."[32] A critical part of what was needed was religious mediation between "the pluralism of Protestants, Catholics, and Jews, or perhaps more fundamentally the basic dichotomy between the religious and the secularists."[33] Although Hesburgh recognized that a unique communion bound all people who professed faith in Christ, he also believed the work of mediation was needed between people who professed faith in God and even people who professed no faith in God.

In many ways, Vatican II enhanced Hesburgh's commitment to the work of mediation and the unique role the Catholic university could play in such efforts. By March 1966, Notre Dame hosted the "International Conference on the Theology of Vatican II."[34] When Hesburgh addressed the gathering, he referred to Vatican II as "the greatest theological event in the Western hemisphere in our times,"[35] and he noted that living theology, the kind inspired by the council, was "the best proof for mankind that God is not dead."[36]

According to Hesburgh, "The Catholic university's key task in an evolving modern society is one of mediation,"[37] and the conference was a critical effort to that end. Such a place and such a topic demanded an appreciation for "standing between all extremes as a bridge, encouraging traffic from all directions, providing a welcome for good ideas from whatever source, [and] being a place for pilgrims: where all can listen, speak, argue, discuss, dialogue, and hopefully, learn."[38] Hesburgh believed the Catholic university was such a place and could build upon the fact that "theological and biblical revival are key realities in our day, as are amicable discussions between great theologians who have begun to talk to each other after four centuries of silence, broken only by noisy polemic."[39]

Hesburgh also took this message concerning mediation and ecumenism directly to leaders of Protestant colleges and universities at their 1967 annual meeting in Los Angeles. A large part of Hesburgh's message was a response to Harvey Cox, a theologian from Harvard Divinity School, and Cox's argument concerning the advantageous nature of the ongoing secularization of colleges and universities.[40] Responding to Cox, Hesburgh contended that "the mediation of God's message to every age must somehow go on, and it is precisely to do this work of mediation that Christian colleges and universities were founded and exist today."[41]

When focusing more directly on the centrality of the mediation of God's message to ecumenism, Hesburgh exhorted his Protestant contemporaries to be "ready to mediate Christ's message to all forms of human knowledge in institutions sympathetic to the message, our Christian colleges and universities, and outside them, too, within the broader collegiate and university context. Ours is not the concept of a ghetto, but a leaven and a light in the darkness."[42] That message, and the hope it offered to the world, was what made their institutions unique. Hesburgh challenged leaders of those institutions not only to do whatever they could to cultivate an appreciation of that message. They also needed to do whatever they could to help their colleagues explore the ramifications of that message with anyone they encountered. Some may listen; some may not. Regardless, their calling was to be a "leaven and a light in the darkness."

Toward the end of his address, Hesburgh sought to reinforce the significance of such efforts they could pursue in common. When doing so, he even argued, "We should indeed disaffiliate ourselves from any influence that is not ecumenical, that cuts us off from each other or from the world, or from the very real values that are to be derived from a wider understanding of all the social revolutions in progress."[43] Hesburgh was not contending that his gathered colleagues should disaffiliate themselves from other leaders who harbor such views. In contrast, he was urging them to search their own hearts and minds for anything that might keep them from joining in the advancement of ecumenical relations.

A VISION FOR THE AGE

Looking back in 1969, Hesburgh said, "When Pope John opened the windows, it wasn't just fresh air that blew in—it was a major hurricane."[44] Vatican II was a force of creative disruption for the Church. "Change [had] so modified the Church and all of the institutions within it that many who converted to the Church because of its seemingly changeless style of life, down to the use of a dead language [e.g., Mass in Latin], are now having second thoughts about their decision."[45] As previously echoed, Hesburgh was one who supported change, especially if it was rooted in something greater than the whims of fashion. He also realized that the changes inspired by Vatican II made visionary leadership necessary.

When speaking before the 1969 annual convention of the National Catholic Educational Association in Detroit, Michigan, Hesburgh contended, "Good management used to be enough." But "today, what is needed as well is vision and this is a reasonably rare human quality. Without vision, the good leadership of normal times becomes hesitant and worried. Change is seen as totally destructive of all that is secure and good and given, rather than an opportunity to update, to develop, or to reassess."[46] Echoing the importance of mediation, Hesburgh then said such vision was necessary to "look ahead rather than only looking back" while also addressing "outmoded dichotomies" such as the "sacred and the profane."[47] In the wake of Vatican II and in the spirit of ecumenism it cultivated, leaders needed to inspire in others a vision for mediation between the past and the present as well as the eternal and the temporal.

According to Hesburgh, leaders also needed to depend on three sets of partners to accomplish such a vision for mediation: "trustees, faculty, and students."[48] In relation to trustees, Hesburgh believed they were "no less Catholic than we [members of a religious order]; sometimes possibly more so." Their diverse array of experiences also ushered in an understanding that "professionalism is the new emphasis, not blind and often uncomprehending or mechanical or unmotivated obedience." Hesburgh believed the institution was now "vastly better off in every way."[49]

Referring to faculty members, Hesburgh noted that the laypeople now serving on the faculties of Catholic schools of higher education had enhanced expectations defining the university as "professionalism and competence are the coin[s] of this realm."[50] Some of those faculty members were not Catholic but members of other Christian traditions. In his estimation, "they made ecumenism a reality in Catholic institutions of higher learning long before most people knew what the word meant." Many of those same faculty members, despite not being Catholic, "cherished everything that the word Catholic, at its best, stands for. They are at home with us and we have had a better home of the intellect because of their presence."[51] Such faculty members could contribute and even enhance the Catholic mission of the university.

Finally, Hesburgh acknowledged that the current generation of students, particularly in the late 1960s, posed considerable challenges to leaders. Hesburgh pointed out their "difficult, demanding, [and] revolutionary" nature. He also acknowledged that without students, "there would be little reason for our institutions"[52] and that those restless qualities set an array of opportunities before educators, as this generation expected relevance, involvement, and service to be outgrowths of their education. Hesburgh argued, "Here again, the Catholic college and university can lead the way amid shifting sands, if we have the courage to insist that there are philosophical and theological realities, bearing on the nature and destiny of man, that have a much longer half-life, in fact a life stretching into eternity."[53] Many students were Catholics, but Catholic colleges and universities were now attracting students from widening circles of faith traditions. Regardless, Hesburgh's vision led him to believe all students could benefit from wisdom rooted in sources with a much longer half-life than many beckoning for their attention.

Hesburgh also shared the importance of an ecumenical vision with his own colleagues at Notre Dame. For example, when addressing the faculty in October 1985, he began by reviewing how the university had grown since its founding by Father Edward Sorin in 1842. In particular, he noted the university recently experienced unprecedented growth on several fronts. Even so, he believed "a perspective reflecting vision and faith is no less important" now than in previous decades.[54] In relation to that vision, Hesburgh acknowledged that "Catholics, Christians, and non-Christians, share the dream of all this Catholic university can yet become." He went so far as to argue "that many non-Catholic and non-Christian members of our faculty and students have been more dedicated to the basic values and aims of this University than some Catholics have."[55]

Even after his retirement from the presidency, Hesburgh continued to stress this important theme, of vison in an age of ecumenism. For example, when delivering a lecture at Emory University in October 1988, he unpacked the active and contemplative examples of lived faith by exploring the lives of Martin Luther King Jr. and the Trappist monk Thomas Merton. Although "both began the campaign focusing on civil rights in America," Hesburgh noted that King "was on the battle line" while Merton was "behind the lines."[56] Even so, Hesburgh contended King and Merton were not different "in their fidelity to divine inspiration and grace, not in the courage and vision that brought them from obscurity to worldwide attention."[57] Both experienced a "conversion of heart"[58] that fostered within them a vision of justice for the world.

OPEN HEARTS AND MINDS

Based on a vison firmly grounded in (1) the theological reality of the world yet to come and (2) the challenges facing one here and now, Hesburgh believed the age of ecumenism called for an opening of hearts and minds. Consider, for example, the context of the Catholic university. He believed that to be totally free, the institution needed to clarify its commitments. In a 1968 address, Hesburgh argued that the time had come for the Catholic university to be "what it purports to be: a true full-fledged university that is also Catholic; a university that is at once committed and free."[59] Stemming from Vatican II and its call to ecumenism, Hesburgh contended the committed and free university is

> the very quintessence of the pilgrim Church in the intellectual order, seeking answers to ultimate questions in concert with all men of intelligence and good will, drawing on all knowledge and every way of knowing and, especially, bringing every philosophical and theological insight to bear upon the monumental task at hand, whatever the source of these insights.[60]

To open its hearts and minds to the world, the Church and the university as its intellectual agent must first know what commitments define them. Only then can they be free to engage the world regardless of whatever challenge may need attention.

In subsequent addresses, Hesburgh further refined what he meant by openness, how such an understanding differed from the common understanding, and how it applied to both the Church and Catholic university in an age of ecumenism. When speaking before the National Convention of the Catholic Press Association in Denver, Colorado, in 1974, Hesburgh contended that "by opening Vatican Council II, Pope John, in fact opened the Church. He also opened it to the other Christian churches which had not even been called churches before." John

XXIII "introduced modesty, receptiveness, listening, [and] in a word, openness."[61] As a result, Hesburgh believed, "the Catholic university is more at ease in the Catholic Church today than ever before."[62] Openness can persist because Vatican II and the age of ecumenism it initiated cultivated an understanding that "we all face the future together in faith, hope, and love."[63]

Finally, Hesburgh went so far as to argue that "in a true Catholic university, all the doors should be open, and the windows, too."[64] When addressing the audience gathered for Duquesne University's centennial celebration on October 3, 1978, Hesburgh argued that all universities claim to pursue truth "but that the Catholic university is even more committed because of its faith and search for grace." With those commitments in place, the mediatory role of the Catholic university made it "closed to none, open to all, seated in time, yearning for eternity, a pilgrim institution with a pilgrim's faith and hope and love."[65]

◊ ◊ ◊

On August 6, 1964, Paul VI issued *Ecclesiam Suam* (His Own Church). With the council fathers preparing to return to Rome for the third session of Vatican II, Paul VI was quick to note in his first encyclical that his purpose for writing was "merely to send you a sincere message, as between brothers and members of a common family" (*Ecclesiam Suam* 7).[66] That message contained three principal policies of his pontificate that he hoped would animate the council's remaining deliberations: self-knowledge, renewal, and dialogue. One could argue that Vatican II is too recent a historical event to allow for a full assessment of its impact. As Matthew Levering, a theologian at Mundelein Seminary, noted, Vatican II is still an ongoing theological event.[67] However, the spirit of Paul VI's three principal policies is imprinted on the constitutions the council drafted and how many religious and laypeople interpreted them.

Hesburgh viewed his mediating role in relation to ecumenism as identifying and practicing spiritual elements that brought people together. He hoped the Tantur Ecumenical Institute would serve as a space where such elements would be put into practice. He also hoped the words he wrote and spoke—words concerning the need for vision as well as open hearts and open minds—would have a lasting impact on Catholics, Orthodox, and Protestants alike. All the while, he labored so that the solidarity of the Church could increase "until the day it will be brought to perfection."

CHAPTER 5

COMMITMENT, COMPASSION, AND CONSECRATION

Our Lord once said that we must lose our lives to gain them. The compassionate lose themselves in helping others, but in a real sense, they are the only moderns who really learn who they are, what they cherish, what makes their lives rich beyond accounting.

—Theodore M. Hesburgh, CSC
The Hesburgh Papers, *1979*

David Gaus, an accounting major and senior from Milwaukee, was undergoing a vocational crisis. He was good at accounting, and in the Gaus family accounting was what one did. As graduation drew closer, Gaus sensed his calling was elsewhere, but where, exactly, he did not know. For counsel, Gaus turned to Hesburgh who was in the final years of his presidency and whose open-door policy had become legendary among students. As they talked, Hesburgh proposed that Gaus serve in a family development program in Quito, Ecuador, evaluate his experience, and then decide. With his degree in accounting and an emerging passion not to walk away from people needing his assistance, Gaus moved to Quito. Awaiting him there was an experience that would not only change his life but the lives of thousands he would encounter in the coming decades.

For Hesburgh, the calling that individuals such as David Gaus embraced was

> to mediate between what is and what might be with the grace of God; to stand between the hope of salvation and the despair of damnation, to uphold the ideal, even though the real is dismal; to work and sacrifice and pray and not despair or give up—because the good news has been announced long ago by the good Lord and we in this day have the great and noble task of proclaiming it anew.[1]

On both theoretical and practical levels, Hesburgh's understanding of economic development knew no boundary between the eternal and the temporal. On the theoretical level, economic development was about being an agent of grace and doing what one can to redeem the conditions under which all too many people live. On the practical level, Hesburgh insisted that economic development was a complex matter that demanded individuals consider a host of conditions.

Those conditions, however, were not limited to improving one's immediate financial situation. In contrast, those conditions related to anything that diminished the image of God born by all people. One's immediate financial situation was often critical and an inextricable part of the challenge. Access to clean water, nutritious food, suitable health care, safe working conditions, fair wages, and more, were also parts of how he viewed economic development. Addressing any one of those challenges may lead one to realize that reality is, in fact, dismal. As the Church's public intellectual, however, Hesburgh believed Christ's crucifixion, as reenacted each day in celebrating the Mass, made the hope for something better not merely wishful thinking but a concrete reality, a reality in which all who serve in Christ's name were called to participate.

LOGICAL, CONTROVERSIAL, AND REVOLUTIONARY

For Hesburgh, that mediatory role, that calling to participate in the hope the crucifixion made possible, led him to serve in ways some found logical, some found controversial, and still others found revolutionary. Over the course of his lifetime, Hesburgh focused considerable time and energy addressing the role the United States could play in worldwide economic development. For example, "During the Johnson years, [he] served briefly on the Commission to Study International Development in the Third World (the Perkins Commission) and on the Policy Planning Board of the State Department."[2] As noted in chapter 2, Hesburgh also served on the United Nations Conference on Science and Technology for Development.

On a more controversial note, at the same time Hesburgh chaired the Overseas Development Council, he chaired the Rockefeller Foundation. Although his service with the private Overseas Development Council did not prove controversial, his service with the Rockefeller Foundation did, especially as he denounced abortion as being in opposition to Catholic teaching that sought to uphold life. The Rockefeller Foundation did not directly participate in the practice of providing abortion services but funded entities that did, such as Planned Parenthood. As part of its efforts to address global poverty, the Rockefeller Foundation also funded population-related studies.[3] Hesburgh justified his service with the Rockefeller Foundation based on the totality of the foundation's efforts, not on efforts that represented relatively small portions of its budget.

Finally, Hesburgh and the University of Notre Dame were directly involved in the revolutionary effort that came to be known as the Peace Corps, a program that called "upon young Americans to enlist for two years of service abroad in the underdeveloped countries of the world." Hesburgh believed the Peace Corps "was a brilliant idea, just the kind of thing the country needed. It was a period when America's reputation as leader of the free world was declining and many of our own young people needed a constructive outlet—for their own pent-up idealism."[4] Heading the effort to launch the Peace Corps was Sargent Shriver, president of the Catholic Interracial Council and brother-in-law to John F. Kennedy, and Harris Wofford, who served as Hesburgh's legal aide with the Civil Rights Commission.

Shriver asked Hesburgh if Notre Dame could provide the Peace Corps with a pilot project. Hesburgh replied that Notre Dame would. In fact, the university already had relationships through the Congregation of Holy Cross with possible host nations such as Bangladesh and Chile. With Chile chosen for the site of the pilot project, Shriver expressed to Hesburgh concern about the "Catholic factor," as Shriver, Hesburgh, and Kennedy were Catholic, "and the project had been put together by a group of Catholics at a Catholic university." As a result, Hesburgh persuaded the Indiana Conference of Higher Education to sponsor the pilot project at Notre Dame. "Anglicans, Lutherans, Baptists, Presbyterians, Mennonites, and Fundamentalists of all kinds" supported "a non-sectarian Peace Corps."[5]

A COMPLEX COMPOSITION

With his economic development colleagues, Hesburgh reiterated the theme that efforts such as the Peace Corps needed to be prepared to navigate "a complex composite of many historical, cultural, social, economic, political, and geographic facts."[6] Underscoring his remark was that approximately one-third of the world's population lived in countries that had only recently achieved nationhood. Although each county had its own reason, Hesburgh argued that

> this coming of nationhood was accompanied by a great growth in national consciousness, a new hope for a better life on the part of millions of people, a hunger for education as the key to tomorrow's hopes for a better social, economic, and cultural condition, and, most importantly,

the firm conviction that political independence would soon bring all of these blessings.[7]

That rapidly changing identity, compounded by the fact that each nation had a unique history and set of reasons for seeking political independence, meant economic development efforts demanded attention to a wide-ranging set of details. Regardless, what united these nations is they "all have the same aspiration for a better life."[8]

When contemplating economic development efforts, Hesburgh was quick to note that "one of the greatest dangers at this time is the temptation to espouse a single answer to all of the needs of the less developed world."[9] An effort that benefited people in one nation is not guaranteed to benefit people in another. However, "while avoiding the temptation of the simple univocal answer," one may be able to discern "that there are elements common to every possible solution"— elements such as economic and political stability, raising educational standards, and increasing agricultural efficiency, to name a few. "Material development creates a condition in which human dignity is possible, we know that man does not live by bread alone."[10]

Hesburgh believed that scholars populating universities should be among the leading proponents addressing the challenges of economic development facing so many nations. Speaking in 1964 to the Interfederal Assembly of Pax Romana in Washington, DC, Hesburgh contended "that universities, new and old, and university people, young and old, must address themselves to this new task with a sense of urgency, born of the urgency of the problem itself, and the centrality of the university world in any reasonable solution."[11] Due to the general shortage of resources with which universities were operating in these contexts, Hesburgh proposed faculty and student exchange programs as valued means of drawing like-minded people together to address these challenges. Hesburgh went on to argue that faculty and students in areas such as science and technology, economics, business, sociology, political science, history, philosophy, and theology all had roles to play in relation to the complex nature of the challenges facing these nations.

Drawing upon his understanding of Christian anthropology, Hesburgh continued, "Development in this context must be relevant to man's nature and destiny, in eternity as well as in time, for it is the total man who is both the subject and object of development." What could unite such efforts, as a result, was "the basic principle of human dignity, inherent and inalienable in man since he receives it in his very nature as a creature made in the image and likeness of the Eternal God."[12]

Four months later, at the Council of Graduate Schools' annual meeting in Chicago, Hesburgh revisited many of those ideas but in ways applicable to that audience. The age in which they lived was one of rapid change. Although Hesburgh said he welcomed change, he also argued change was not inherently good. In contrast, change must be guided by the outcome of a relationship shared with human emancipation, human development, and technological innovation.

To embrace such a vision for change, Hesburgh argued "universities should be international." He believed he and his colleagues "must serve the whole of humanity [and] become more learned and hence more free." Although domestic students needed access to ample opportunities to study abroad, "our doors should be as wide open as possible to international, let us stop calling them foreign, students."[13] Only then could universities properly invest in the complex array of challenges facing nations in relation to economic development.

In his baccalaureate address at Indiana University nearly a year later, Hesburgh made a comparable plea to the assembled graduates. He opened again by noting "this is one of the most revolutionary of all ages of mankind—mainly because we are in the midst of unprecedented changes, the rapidity of which change, and the magnitude of people affected by the change being without parallel in the history of mankind."[14]

He again argued that change must be guided by a shared relationship between human emancipation, human development, and technological innovation. Perhaps now more than ever before, economic development was a possible yet complicated reality. As with his colleagues who guided graduate education, Hesburgh asked the students, "Are you willing to get involved?"[15] If so, involvement would demand commitment, compassion, and consecration. Those demands might lead them to serve close to home. However, in the rapidly changing world in which those students lived, they might be led to serve far afield.

IDENTITY AND ACTION

Hesburgh emphasized another theme in relation to economic development—that one's identity as a person relates to the course of action one chooses to follow. For example, when addressing graduates at the University of Wyoming in 1964, Hesburgh opened by arguing,

> Up to this point in your lives, everyone else has been working to help you to be someone worthwhile. But while others can *do* for you, no one can *be* for you. Now is the time for you to assess what has happened: what and who you are, and what in turn you can now do for yourself, your country, and your world. But, I stress again, before you can *do* something, you must *be* something.[16]

The world was changing rapidly, and the array of needs beckoning for the attention of college graduates was great. Hesburgh believed individuals were to spend their lives mediating between the eternal beauty of what the world could be and the all-too-often dismal nature of what the world presently offered, but they could not do so unless they were sure in their identity.

The answer was different for each person, but Hesburgh articulated some basic points of encouragement. For example, he encouraged Wyoming graduates to respect themselves, be passionate about justice, and commit themselves "to a cause that transcends your own convenience or comfort."[17] He then turned to a component of the Christian anthropology that defined so many of his ideas. He argued that "the quality of life in America is largely dependent upon our ability to share our blessings with others less fortunate. Our Lord highlights this by saying that we must lose our life to gain it, that it is more blessed to give than receive."[18]

When making a similar argument two years later at the University of Michigan's Institute for Social Research, Hesburgh turned to a now-frequent source in Jacques Maritain and a new one in Barbara Ward, a British intellectual and expert in economic development, to support his claims. Although Hesburgh recognized that the social sciences were valuable partners in advancing economic development for millions, he also saw inherent challenges. For example, Hesburgh believed that simply embracing the "title of science" raised the possibilities of "the amassing of data for the sake of data, the attempt to quantify the unquantifiable, the cult of mathematical verification in an effort to establish theories ultimately beyond mathematics, [and] the worship of objectivity to an extent that [it] often sterilized what might have been very fruitful research."[19]

To avoid these challenges while also reaping the benefits of what the social sciences could offer economic development, Hesburgh encouraged his audience to recognize that "the process of investigating a social science problem represents something worthwhile or useless, and the conclusions resulting are something of value or not, depending upon a whole series of real value judgments all along the line of research. To say then that the social scientist is not interested in values is, to me at least, nonsense."[20]

As echoed in relation to scientists in chapter 2, Hesburgh urged social scientists to be aware of their values, evaluate them critically, and put them to use in terms of defining the purpose of their research. "Without values," Hesburgh argued, "there is no science, no discernment, no judgment, no relevance, and certainly no meaningful relationship between social science and the age of social revolution in which we live."[21]

To support such a challenge, Hesburgh once again turned to Jacques Maritain's *Principles of a Humanistic Philosophy*. Whether or not a person recognizes them, every person operates with certain anthropological assumptions. Maritain's—and Hesburgh's—Christian anthropology rested on the conviction that "Spirit is the root of personality." As a result, each person is "animated and activated" by a divine fire from the womb to the grave that exists "by virtue of the very existence of his soul, which dominates time and death."[22] Individuals such as social scientists should thus align their efforts to aid in the "revolution of human equality, for human development, for an end to poverty, the hunger, the illness, the ignorance, the homelessness, the utter hopelessness that afflict so many persons today."[23]

Introducing a larger context in which such efforts take place, Hesburgh pointed audience members to the work of Barbara Ward, particularly the series of lectures eventually published in 1966 in *Spaceship Earth*. In that work, Ward contended, "Modern science and technology have created so close a network of communication, transport, economic interdependence—and potential nuclear destruction—that planet earth, on its journey through infinity, has acquired the intimacy, the fellowship, and the vulnerability of a spaceship." As a result, Ward believed, "there must be rules for survival."[24] Hesburgh then endorsed her arguments as ones that do "not indulge in nationalistic or selfish concerns" and "make sense, in view of the evidence."[25] Similarly, Hesburgh believed the web of relations in which humans existed was too interdependent to fail to pursue economic development not merely for the few but for as many as possible.

IN AN AGE OF CIVIL UNREST

Shortly after Hesburgh gave that address at the University of Michigan, campuses across the country faced unprecedented forms of civil unrest. In an admittedly "oversimplified and possibly overstated"[26] estimation of the challenge, Hesburgh claimed the economic and educational prosperity young people were afforded also gave them clearer access to the disparities defining a nation that publicly prized equality. Participation in the civil rights movement granted them a "new confidence in the rightness of their cause, new power in what they were able to achieve by protest and organized action against what they knew to be wrong, much less un-American." Various dimensions of the Vietnam War, such as "draft cards, ROTC, Dow and napalm, induction centers, troop trains, and military recruiters," led students to a new target for their frustrations: the university.[27]

Instead of viewing such unrest as a challenge to society in general and efforts being made in relation to economic development, Hesburgh viewed it as an opportunity. Just hours after Robert Kennedy died in a Los Angeles hospital in June 1968 from wounds inflicted by an assassin, Hesburgh took the podium at the University of Southern California as the university's commencement speaker. When opening that address, Hesburgh acknowledged he visited with the Kennedy family just prior to his arrival on campus and that he understood the mounting urgency many of them felt for a revolution. Instead of many who believed that the mounting urgency was a threat, Hesburgh viewed such urgency was an opportunity as "the world needs energy, imagination, concern, idealism, dedication, commitment, [and] service." If channeled in sustained and peaceful ways, a revolution, "in which justice is available to all," was possible.[28]

Approximately a year later, Hesburgh gave the commencement address at Saint Louis University. After once again noting the desire for revolution amongst some students on many campuses, he acknowledged that leaders "are altogether too concerned with mere methods of maintaining law and order in the university, without being equally concerned about the greater achievement of justice and equality of opportunity in our times."[29] Hesburgh then asked students to join him in forgoing "riot and violent revolution"[30] in favor of addressing "the burning issues of war and peace, human rights, equality and justice for all, the abolition of poverty in the midst of affluence, [and] the eradication of hopelessness and hunger in a land of promise and plenty."[31] Economic development for all was possible, but only if young and old link arms in a common cause to recognize the full humanity of all people.

VATICAN II AND SPACESHIP EARTH

As mentioned in the previous chapter, Hesburgh viewed Vatican II as a valuable contribution to the Church's ability to fulfill its mission and, in turn, link arms with all who sought to mediate between the eternal and the temporal in Christ's name. In Paul VI, Hesburgh found a pope who "more radically changed the system of the Curia than any dozen of his predecessors since the Curia began."[32] When speaking at the National Federation of Priests' Councils in 1971, Hesburgh argued his "proudest boast is that for the better part of the past 28 years I have been a practicing priest, one who loves to celebrate Mass every day as the greatest act of priesthood for the salvation of the whole world."[33]

However, his calling, a calling that included addressing "human development around the world through economic programs and [the] Peace Corps," was "in large measure…lived among the gentiles, largely in gentile endeavors, but with apostolic overtones."[34] In many ways, he viewed Vatican II as confirmation of how he was called to live—somewhere between the glimpse of eternity he gained each day when celebrating Mass and the realities of the temporal world.

As a result, he reaffirmed for his fellow priests that "being an apostle demands of the priest that he first be a servant of Jesus Christ and then a servant to all his people—who are all people—by the special services of hard work of all kinds, prayer, suffering, correction, and even raising money for good causes." Hesburgh then acknowledged that he loathed raising money, but that "St. Paul's epistles were full of it."[35] What the Church needed to cultivate was a vision of leadership predicated on a "vision of Christ and His good news, His Salvific message, that vivifies the Christian community, age after age, and gives new life and continual inspiration to every priest in every age."[36] Such leadership animates the Church and the relationship the Church shares with the world, regardless of the challenge.

That vision for the priesthood and where it might lead brought Hesburgh to Cambridge, Massachusetts, in the spring of 1973, where he delivered the commencement address at Harvard University. Emboldened by his understanding of the life he was to live among the Gentiles and how such a life contributed to economic development, Hesburgh introduced the graduating class to Barbara Ward's recent work via an address he titled "A New Vision for Spaceship Earth." He opened by claiming that although we are all passengers on such a spacecraft, one out of five members of the crew consume four-fifths of the ship's life-sustaining resources. He asked, "How much human peace can you visualize or expect aboard our spaceship when its limited resources are so unjustly shared, especially when the situation is worsening each year?" As a priest he was called to claim, "Peace is not gained by armaments but by justice."[37]

Following Ward's lead, Hesburgh proposed to his audience that they at least think of themselves as individuals who bear the responsibilities of both national and international citizenship. Doing so would afford "each of us with a chance to declare our interdependence with one another, our common humanity, our shared hopes for our spaceship earth, our brotherhood as members of the crew, our common vision of the task facing humanity—to achieve human dignity and the good life together."[38]

Hesburgh's mediatory calling compelled him to conclude that he was prepared on that "day to declare myself a citizen of the world," as he was "first and foremost a priest." He ended by praying "that the good Lord Jesus who lived and died for us may also bless these living efforts of ours to be truly followers of Him who blessed both the peacemakers and all who hunger for justice."[39]

Perhaps the economic development of that interdependent world, the world in which Hesburgh was called to live as a priest, was nowhere more immediately vulnerable than the food supply needed to sustain it. At the 1973 National Conference of Catholic Bishops meeting in

Washington, DC, Hesburgh opened by asserting that "Interdependence is involved in every current discussion of world development, trade, or monetary policy." He referred to interdependence as "a kind of modern Copernican revolution that involves a new way of looking at our world."[40] What that revolution offered, however, was "useful only if translated into the world of reality, to help understand real problems, to elaborate realistic solutions, to change mentalities and cast world views into a more meaningful perspective for a better world." In that context, "the global food problem … is present, urgent, and itself interdependent upon other global problems."[41]

Driving Hesburgh's concern was not only the fact that some members of the planet had too little to eat, but also that "climactic change has had a disastrous effect on food production." In addition, climate change was taking place in locales where food production was already in a fragile state. For example, "the Sahara Desert is moving south at about 30 miles a year," threatening new regions of the continent in terms of their abilities to feed their respective populations.[42] Referencing a now familiar metaphor in Spaceship Earth, Hesburgh claimed that what was needed was a new "world perspective based upon the interdependence of all mankind on this relatively small spacecraft with very finite life resources."[43]

NATIONALS AND MULTINATIONALS

Resistance to his vision—embracing a world perspective based upon interdependence—neither shocked nor deterred Hesburgh. Always looming was "the agony of human perversion that somehow resists the better urgings of our spirit." He persisted, however, in asking "with St. Paul, 'Who will deliver me from the body of this death?' I trust that we will be ready to accept the same answer that St. Paul received, 'The grace of God through Our Lord, Jesus Christ.'"[44] As a result, Hesburgh was willing to take his message of economic development in an interdependent world to at least three sets of institutions poised to make a difference.

First, as early as the Terry Lectures he delivered at Yale University in 1974, Hesburgh argued that nations and the people they governed needed to think of themselves as citizens of the world. Citing Barbara Ward, Hesburgh argued,

> We, the passengers of Spaceship Earth, are capable of creating by our intelligence and freedom a whole series of man-made systems that will enhance the inherent beauty of the planet and make it even more humanly viable. Or we can turn Spaceship Earth into an ugly wasteland where human beings barely survive and hardly live in any human sense.[45]

When deciding how people treat their spaceship, Hesburgh noted national sovereignty was "perhaps the worst of all" dividers.[46] As he contended a year earlier while delivering the commencement address at Harvard University, Hesburgh now argued for the value of dual citizenship—one as a citizen of a nation and one as a citizen of the world. Holding those two forms of citizenship in tension would keep leaders of nations from being shortsighted about the impact of their decisions upon both present and future populations.

Second, Hesburgh expounded upon this message with leaders of multinational corporations in a November 1978 address titled "Multinational Managers and Poverty in the Third World." Hesburgh opened by returning to his argument that economic development is complex. He then noted, "Moreover, there is no simple way of passing judgment on what multinationals are doing"[47] in relation to economic development. Regardless, leaders of such entities have a responsibility to wade into both matters, to think through how their companies are dependent on others and about how others are dependent on their companies. Toward the end of his address, Hesburgh argued, "Multinationals have understood interdependence perhaps better than any other entity in the world,"[48] referring to their ability to communicate and transfer funds, people, technology across a multitude of cultures. He now challenged them with the opportunity to think through "what should be one's responsibility towards social justice, both internally within the company and externally."[49]

Finally, Hesburgh presented that message to his fellow leaders of universities. When speaking at the College of William and Mary's 287th Charter Day in 1980, for example, he argued that the purpose of a liberal education was to make one free. However, the freedom he envisioned was "a balance between our individual and social good, our particular and communal well-being, our happiness fundamentally, as human persons and as a human society."[50] A liberal education should teach humans to situate themselves. When doing so, students should learn their well-being as people was inextricably tied on several levels to the well-being of others.

◊ ◊ ◊

Haunted by what he witnessed in Quito during the two years he lived there, Gaus was fueled by a calling to meet the medical needs of the Ecuadorian people. That calling compelled him to take the basic science courses he needed to gain admission to medical school at Tulane University. After medical school, Gaus returned to Ecuador and established a health-care system from which the population living in the rural north, a population often afflicted by poverty, could receive local care. Now known as Andean Health and Development (AHD), the system Gaus established includes two hospitals and a residency program that trains "family physicians to become the rural health care leaders of tomorrow." AHD is now financially self-sustaining and through its residency program is self-perpetuating, "staffed with 100% local Ecuadorians."[51]

About three and a half hours west of Quito resides the community of Santo Domingo. Despite having a population of three hundred thousand and being the seat of the canton bearing its name, Santo Domingo de los Colorados, Santo Domingo's health-care infrastructure was incapable of meeting the short- and long-terms needs of its population. In 2014, Gaus and his colleagues, however, opened their second hospital (the first an hour and a half away in Pedro Vicente Maldonado), a facility in Santo Domingo featuring "60 beds, comprehensive health services, residency training programs for family Physicians, and a research and resource center."[52] When speaking at the hospital's dedication, Gaus echoed the mediatory spirit of his mentor and AHD's first board chair when he claimed,

> This hospital symbolizes hope—the hope that we can really bring about change in the way health care is done and that utopia is really worth fighting for—one that all people, rich and poor, regardless of their ethnicity, when they suffer from illness, that they have access to high-quality health care services.[53]

The name of Santo Domingo's newest hospital? Hospital Hesburgh.

CHAPTER 6

THE GOOD OF THE PEOPLE

As long as there is a contradiction of abundance for the few and utter hopelessness for the many, the many are going to move wherever there is abundance. You in your lifetime may yet see tens of millions of starving people marching to where there is food.

—*Theodore M. Hesburgh, CSC*
Commencement Address, University of Michigan, 1981

At approximately 8:30 a.m. on Wednesday, August 7, 2019, Dr. Tony McGee, the superintendent for Scott County Public Schools, learned that day was not going to be routine. Just the previous day, McGee and his colleagues survived both the excitement and chaos that comes with the first day of the school year. Students had now found their classes, met their teachers, and decided with whom they were going to eat lunch. In the school district approximately forty-five minutes east of Jackson, Mississippi, Wednesday was supposed to be the day when educators and students alike started settling into the year's routine.

Federal officials, however, had other plans. According to the *Scott County Times*,

> Peco Foods in Sebastopol [MS], the Koch Foods plant in Morton [MS] and PH Food in Morton were all part of the

coordinated raids. All three plants were shut down for the entire day while federal agents from HSI [Homeland Security Investigations] and ICE [Immigration and Customs Enforcement] took illegal immigrants and unauthorized workers into custody and transported them off-site to a processing center.[1]

PBS NewsHour noted that those raids were part of "the largest single state action of its kind in U.S. history."[2] The Scott County Times reported that ICE officials "ultimately netted 680 illegal or undocumented employees in the state."[3] Scott was not the only county in central Mississippi that witnessed raids on that day, but the county of thirty thousand people was impacted in incalculable ways.

The calls started pouring into McGee's office shortly after the raids occurred, indicating that parents of some Scott County students might be among the detainees. As a result, he and his colleagues spent the day identifying affected students. McGee said he then talked "directly with the ICE agent in charge to inform them about our children in school and to find out if the parents would be released. We wanted to ensure that none of our children would be in need or without a parent, caregiver or guardian."[4]

Before August 7, 2019, Scott County, Mississippi, was not a flashpoint in national debates about immigration. However, the events of that day and the ones that followed added Scott County to the growing list of locales upon which those discussions are centered. When talking with PBS Newshour's Jeffrey Brown, McGee noted, "On our end, especially in the community and the schools, we had no prior knowledge so it was—it was pretty—pretty shocking. It was really a tough day emotionally for educators and students and families."[5]

Unfortunately, the present cycle of debate concerning immigration was neither the first nor, given the state of divisiveness presently surrounding it, likely the last. In the history of the United States, only two select commissions were charged with addressing this topic. The first commission, appointed by President Theodore Roosevelt, conducted its work from 1907 to 1910. The advice of that commission "was predicated on the assumption that there were superior and inferior races. It wanted immigration mainly from Northern Europe and its advice was reflected in the first formal immigration laws, following World War I in 1921."[6]

The second commission, appointed by President Jimmy Carter, worked from 1979 to 1981. That commission, the Select Commission on Immigration and Refugee Policy, was chaired by Theodore Hesburgh; the five-hundred-page report it submitted to Congress was titled *U.S. Immigration Policy and the National Interest*. In addition to chairing the Select Commission, Hesburgh facilitated several related efforts, such as the pledging of $69 million for relief assistance in Cambodia.[7]

Prior to his appointment by President Carter as chair of the commission, Hesburgh rarely spoke or wrote about immigration, but the well-being of refugees was a pronounced dimension of his work from almost the very beginning. In his 1981 commencement address at the University of Michigan, Hesburgh noted, "Refugees are mainly the children of war, persecution, and drought."[8] Those unfortunate conditions compel people to flee their homes and, in turn, generate discussions elsewhere concerning immigration.

As the Church's public intellectual, Hesburgh viewed his mediating role in relation to refugees and immigration as one by which pathways were created. While the commission focused its efforts on pathways to immigration, Hesburgh also worked on pathways related to the alleviation of challenges refugees faced. In the University of Michigan address, Hesburgh noted the conditions creating refugees are world problems "that desperately need a global solution. The only long range solution is economic and social development in that part of the world where 80% of the world's people have only 20% of the resources available for basic human needs."[9] Conversations concerning immigration policy in one nation would offer only short-term solutions to challenges that ultimately were the result of structural inequities plaguing one if not many other nations.

When speaking to seminarians at the Chicago Archdiocese's Niles College Seminary in May 1986, Hesburgh acknowledged that the call to mediate between what the world was created to be and the present challenges the world faced could prove overwhelming. He pointed to the challenges of "world hunger, refugees, and immigration"[10] being among the most pressing and thus the worthiest of the Church's attention. However, Hesburgh was quick to remind his colleagues that although they had roles to play, solutions to those challenges were not dependent on their force of will. In contrast, he pointed them back to Saint Thomas Aquinas, who referred to a priest as a "mediator between God and man." They then fulfilled their calling by offering Christ's "good news, love, forgiveness, [and] his grace." Such efforts were thus not dependent on their efforts but their willingness to make Christ "real to our age."[11]

THE SELECT COMMISSION

For Hesburgh, making Christ real to his age was a task that demanded prayerful discernment and divine wisdom when it came to work with refugees and immigration. The root challenge, the one Hesburgh never lost sight of, was tragic sets of circumstances compelled more people each year to flee their homes. In this context, Hesburgh received another phone call, this time from Jimmy Carter's vice president, Walter Mondale. The way Hesburgh told the story, Mondale said, "The President wants you to chair the U.S. Select Commission on Immigration and Refugee Policy....It's only a two year job which you can do in your spare time."[12]

In almost predictable fashion, Hesburgh responded, "I don't know anything about immigration and refugees."[13] Mondale then offered,

> Neither does anyone else. That is why Congress established the Commission with sixteen high level members: The Secretary of State, the Attorney General, the Secretaries of Labor and HEW [Health, Employment, and Welfare (later HHS) Health and Human Services], the Chairmen

of the Senate and House Judiciary Committee[s], Senator [Edward] Kennedy, Congressman [Peter] Rodino, plus three other members from the Senate and House, and four public members.[14]

All Hesburgh had to do was focus the efforts of this group on a complex and divisive topic and then compose "a very difficult report to write … for the President and Congress, due March 1, 1981."[15] Predictably, Hesburgh agreed.

At the commission's first meeting, Hesburgh noted he and his fellow commissioners identified "four fundamental questions" they needed to answer: "1) How many immigrants should be admitted to the United States annually; 2) From where; 3) By what procedures; and 4) What should be the criteria governing the answers to the first three questions?"[16] To answer those questions, the commission held public meetings "from Boston to San Francisco, from San Antonio to Phoenix, and more commission meetings all over Washington and even another trip around the world to study immigration in our Pacific Territories and refugees in the Far East."[17]

As a result, "The commission came to the conclusion that the best way of dissuading excess immigration was to make it difficult, if not impossible, for these people to get jobs here without legal entry papers."[18] In essence, they proposed to Congress that the path to legal immigration be widened but that motivation for many to follow the path to illegal immigration be eliminated. As will be explained in detail later, the possession of legal entry papers would not only guarantee that jobs would go to the most deserving, but also keep employers from taking advantage of illegal immigrants via unfair or even unsafe labor practices.

Realizing no practical way existed for them to meet the full demand for legal immigration, Hesburgh and his colleagues identified three categories by which individuals seeking legal paths to immigration would receive preferential treatment. First, the "main preference" they identified "would be for the reunification of families, mainly spouses and children." The second category granted preferential treatment to "seed immigrants" or individuals who were "looking for economic opportunity, a new life, and a new hope."[19] In many ways, that category was established to honor the history of the United States and why so many individuals had previously sought citizenship. Finally, preference was also granted to refugees or people needing to flee their homes. Obviously, many individuals would qualify for two or three categories.

The proposal offered to Congress came in the form of three interdependent recommendations, which Hesburgh likened to a "tripod, with the understanding that if any leg of the solution is rejected, the other two will not stand." The first recommendation, and one the commission proposed unanimously, was "that the present illegals who have been here since January 1, 1980, and whose record of work and conduct meets the immigrant standard, be given the opportunity to legalize their status, first as permanent alien residents for five years, and then have the opportunity for naturalization as citizens."[20]

As previously echoed, Hesburgh and his colleagues wanted to make sure jobs in the United States went to the most deserving workers and that those workers were paid a fair wage. At the same time, Hesburgh and his colleagues wanted to protect undocumented individuals from being "under paid, victimized by unscrupulous employers, [and] often paying taxes with no benefits." Allowing such treatment to go unchecked "creates a subculture that depresses labor standards and wages, an unhealthy situation for all our society, especially those caught in this trap."[21]

The second leg of the tripod was to sanction employers who hire individuals not otherwise "legally qualified to work" in the United States. One of the inconsistencies Hesburgh and his colleagues identified in the law at that time was that individuals could not "come into the country illegally and work, but [it was] not illegal for employers to hire them." The responsibility for discerning who was legally eligible to work would now fall squarely on the employer. Hesburgh and his colleagues believed people would cease to come illegally if they knew they had little to no chance of securing employment. They would "demagnify the magnet that brings them here illegally."[22] Such a proposal would also protect employees and ensure they were treated in a fair and humane manner.

Finally, to help employers identify employees legally eligible for employment, the commission proposed issuing "an upgraded and counterfeit-proof Social Security card." The present system depended on papers easy for prospective employees to forge and difficult for employers to confirm. Such a card "is presently held by everyone; it is used for driver's licensing, most official papers, and numerous other identification purposes." Hesburgh and his colleagues believed "it applies to all equally." The change would be the use of "new laser and magnetic technology [that] could make it practically counterfeit-proof and more care could be exerted in issuing new cards."[23]

Optimistic that their tripod of proposals would at least slow if not stem the tide of illegal immigration, Hesburgh and his colleagues proposed that "the front door to America, the legal door, should be opened a bit wider and the back door, the illegal one, closed."[24] Hesburgh recounted that "we recommended widening the front door to immigration—allowing 500,000 legal aliens to enter the United States each year, or about double the 230,000 quota."[25] Political conservatives did not like the first leg of the stool—amnesty. Political liberals did not like the second leg of the stool—confirmation of employment eligibility. The third proposal—issuing federal identification cards— "raised the hackles of the American Civil Liberties Union and similar libertarians who argued vociferously that such identity cards were an invasion of privacy and the first step toward a totalitarian state."[26]

In his 1981 State of the Union Address, Jimmy Carter summarized the challenges facing refugees before giving an update on the efforts of the Select Commission on Immigration and Refugee Policy. The previous year, instability in their home nations led "thousands of Cubans and Haitians [to seek] refuge in our country last year, outside of our regular immigration and refugee admissions process, our country and its government were tested in being compassionate and responsive to a major human emergency." Carter then noted, "Because we had taken steps to reorganize our refugee programs, we met that test successfully. I am proud that the American people responded to this crisis with their traditional good will and hospitality."[27]

In the face of such a challenge, Carter continued, "While we must remain committed to aiding and assisting those who come to our shores, at the same time we must uphold our immigration and refugee policies and provide adequate enforcement resources." After noting that the Select Commission's report was due in March, he hoped "that the recommendations will be carefully considered by the new Administration and the Congress, for it is clear that we must take additional action to keep our immigration policy responsive to emergencies and ever changing times."[28]

According to Hesburgh, Carter's successor, Ronald Reagan, "set up his own fact-finding commission and that commission spent another two years going over the same material, the same issues, the same difficulties as we did, and in the end adopted the same recommendations as we had."[29] The three legs of the tripod were then revised in a number of ways by Congress. However, because of leadership exercised by Senator Alan Simpson (R-Wyoming) and Representative Romano Mazzoli (D-Kentucky), the Immigration Reform and Control Act became law in 1986.

80/20

As previously noted, Hesburgh viewed his mediating role in relation to refugees and immigration as one that considered pathways (1) to immigration and (2) to alleviating the conditions refugees faced. The latter component of his calling surfaced much earlier in his speeches and writing than the former. For example, Hesburgh's concern that "80% of the world's people have only 20% of the resources available for basic human needs,"[30] surfaced as early as 1962 in his MIT commencement address. As detailed in chapter 3, Hesburgh believed part of the challenge facing the development of science and technology was the larger purpose that inspired it.

For all the good science and technology could generate, mere indulgence was also a possibility. Hesburgh recounted for his audience in Cambridge on that day, "I have seen people dying on the streets of Calcutta; I have seen hungry refugee children on the sampans and in the shacks of Hong Kong; I have seen unnecessary disease in Uganda, in Pakistan, in Brazil, and Chile." He then noted he was "slightly nauseated when I see science and technology dedicated to trivial purposes." Science and technology, however, could be "directed against man's ancient enemies of hunger, disease, illness, and ignorance."[31] These enemies of course often compel people to flee their homes.

In the 1970s, the challenge of world hunger and the conditions causing it surfaced more prominently in Hesburgh's work. As early as 1974, Hesburgh referenced climate change as a factor disrupting the food production cycles upon which so many were dependent. As previously mentioned, for example, African nations were witnessing the Sahara "moving south at about 30 miles a year." When delivering the Ditchley Foundation Lecture in the United Kingdom that September, Hesburgh recounted, "In the refugee camps around Nouakshott, Timbuktu, and Gao, one sees thousands of Tuaregs who have lost all of their herds and are despondently dependent on a minimal amount of rice, wheat, and corn flown in daily on military airlifts."[32]

He then noted that in those areas most vulnerable to climate change or "those incredibly torrid and sandy spots, one sees the face of hungry desperation and realizes that human suffering transcends the grim statistics. People starve, and die, not numbers." Part of the challenge facing populations such as the Tuaregs, according to Hesburgh, is that "we in the developed world are consuming almost a ton of food grains annually per person while the poorest billion people in the world barely subsist on 400 pounds a year." Beyond the disparity in the human consumption of grain, Hesburgh noted that "affluence has doubled meat consumption during the past twenty years in America and Canada and throughout the developed world. Since it takes seven pounds of grain to produce one pound of beef, more grains are fed to animals in America than are consumed directly in the poor nations."[33] As a result, the conditions that displace people from their homes are often inseparable from the luxuries people experience elsewhere.

Later in that same speech, Hesburgh noted that many of these disparities exist between nations in the Northern Hemisphere and those in the Southern Hemisphere. For example, "If a child is born in the North, he or she faces an ever-lengthening life characterized by increasing health, education, economic, and social well-being." In contrast, if a child is "born in most of the Southern parts of the globe, he or she will face a short life, illness, illiteracy, hunger, abominable housing, [and] hopelessness." In terms of access to food, "We are often overfed and overweight, they are undernourished from birth, often suffering brain damage."[34] Evidence of these observations resides in patterns of immigration in which refugees often move south to north.

On one level, Hesburgh addressed these challenges by encouraging his audience to think, as detailed in previous chapters, of planet Earth as a spaceship. Following Barbara Ward's lead, Hesburgh contended that when the human population envisions itself inhabiting tighter quarters, the finite nature of available resources becomes more immediately evident as does the disparate nature of the allocation of those resources. In turn, we learn to view the members of the crew as interdependent, not independent. He argued, for example, that "the decision of an Arab sheik, a Japanese industrialist, [or] an American governmental bureaucrat leaves them [other crew members or populations around the world] without irrigation water and fertilizer and, consequently, without food."[35] When the world is viewed as related in such a way, Hesburgh hoped humanity would "look at the new opportunities and creative responses that interdependence would suggest."[36]

On another level, Hesburgh addressed these challenges by again encouraging his audience to think in Christian anthropological terms. While Hesburgh did not reference here the work of Jacques Maritain, he once again turned to texts from Genesis and Matthew. Hesburgh drew from the story of Cain and Abel as found in Genesis 4:9. After

Cain attacked and killed his brother, God asked Cain, "Where is your brother Abel?" In particular, he quoted Cain's response, "Am I my brother's keeper?"

Hesburgh then cited Matthew 25:40, part of a larger passage often referred to as the Judgement of Nations. Here Christ unveiled what determines the differences between the eternally blessed as represented by sheep and the eternally cursed as represented by goats. Christ offered, "Amen, I say to you, whatever you did for one of these least brothers of mine, you did for me." Service to the hungry, the thirsty, the stranger, the naked, or the prisoner is service to Christ.

When "80% of the world's people have only 20% of the resources available for basic human needs," Hesburgh argued that no question existed concerning "who are our least brethren in today's world." He challenged, "The choices are simple and stark: greed or altruism, hatred or love, growing discontinuities or new development, in a word, war or peace."[37]

DIGNITY OF ALL PERSONS

Eight months after the Select Commission on Immigration and Refugee Policy submitted *U.S. Immigration Policy and the National Interest* to Congress, Hesburgh gave an address in New York City to leaders of the American Federation of Labor and Congress of Industrial Organizations (AFL-CIO) in which he offered details on how he thought through immigration policy. Early in his address, he noted that a century earlier, his grandfather had been a columnist in New York City. At the time, "the labor movement was being organized" and the rights of workers to organize were very much in question. His grandfather "valiantly upheld the efforts of the laboring class to organize." As a result, his grandfather "suffered great criticism for his backing [of the labor movement]."[38]

At the same time, the labor movement was being organized and his grandfather was writing, Pope Leo XIII, the author of the first great labor encyclical, *Rerum Novarum*, sent a legate or official representative to New York City "to study the labor movement and the Catholic participation in it." Hesburgh continued, noting that when Leo XIII issued *Rerum Novarum*, his "grandfather's stance was vindicated as he used to tell me proudly when I visited him here in New York City."[39]

As the Select Commission was conducting its work, the Church's new pontiff, John Paul II, was writing what Hesburgh called "another strong labor encyclical—*Laborem Exercens*." Although an assassin's attempt on John Paul II's life in 1981 delayed this encyclical, *Laborem Exercens* was timed to honor the ninetieth anniversary of *Rerum Novarum* and revisit the social issues Leo XIII raised. Hesburgh then noted that a Christian anthropology was central to *Rerum Novarum* that stressed "the worker as a human person, his dignity, his right[s], [and] his fair compensation." In reference to the Reagan administration's economic commitments, Hesburgh offered that the worker's "organizations are all far more important than economics, supply side or any other side."[40]

Ultimately, Hesburgh stressed in that speech to domestic labor leaders that we are "not talking about economic units but about human beings."[41] Hesburgh was a U.S. citizen and volunteered to serve the country that was his geographic home in a number of ways. However, as a priest and member of the Church, Hesburgh also focused on a global set of concerns. By quoting from *Rerum Novarum* before leaders of the AFL-CIO, Hesburgh confirmed that as a priest he was called

> to urge upon men of every class, upon the high-placed as well as the lowly, the Gospel doctrines of Christian life; by every means in their power they must strive to secure the good of the people; and above all must earnestly cherish in themselves, and try to arouse in others, charity, the mistress and the queen of virtues. (no. 63)[42]

Such a calling knew no class or geographic boundary. The Church's universal nature meant its concern was for the dignity of all persons, foreign or domestic.

By quoting from *Laborem Exercens*, Hesburgh reinforced that point in a contemporary key. John Paul II had noted, "We are…on the eve of new developments in technological, economic and political conditions which, according to many experts, will influence the world of work and production no less than the industrial revolution of the last century"; even so, the "Church considers it her task always to call attention to the dignity and rights of those who work, to condemn situations in which that dignity and those rights are violated, and to help to guide the above-mentioned changes so as to ensure authentic progress by man and society" (*Laborem Exercens* 1).[43] As with *Rerum Novarum*, this encyclical makes no mention of citizens of one nation or another, simply "the dignity and rights of those who work."

In "Immigration Reform Five Years Later," Hesburgh exercised the logic put forth in these two encyclicals within the context of efforts made by the Select Commission. At the time, Congress still had not passed immigration reform. Part of Hesburgh's point was to acknowledge once again that the "current immigration policy was inadequate to deal with the growing worldwide migratory pressures." He added, "Immigration reform is, to say the least, a difficult and thorny issue, but one that we can no longer avoid."[44]

After noting the moral dilemma "that gnaws at the conscience of anyone who examines this issue," Hesburgh contended,

> It is not enough to merely sympathize with the aspirations and the plight of illegal aliens. We must also consider the consequences of not controlling our borders. What about the aspirations of Americans who must compete for jobs, and whose wages and standards are depressed by the presence of large numbers of illegal aliens? What about aliens themselves, many of whom are victimized by unscrupulous employers or who die in the desert at the hands of smugglers, America's modern day slave traders?[45]

Any response to this moral dilemma must take into consideration the dignity of all persons, foreign and domestic, and what causes people to flee their homes as well as the policies designed to meet them. In Hesburgh's opinion, all the related components must be addressed.

◊ ◊ ◊

While the 2019–2020 school year in Scott County, Mississippi, maintained its schedule and tried to return to "normal," one wonders about the logic brought to bear on (1) how to serve the needs of refugees and (2) the design and enforcement of immigration policies. Tony McGee and his fellow educators were likely left to help their students make sense of the trauma. Some students may have wondered why their parents were forcibly detained only to be released hours later. Some may have wondered why their parents were forcibly detained and then transferred to a processing center. Still, some may have wondered why parents of their classmates were treated in such a manner. Unfortunately, none of those questions comes with easy answers. As in the late 1970s and early 1980s, Hesburgh would likely argue that what is needed is to "recognize the realities of a tumultuous and impoverished world and maintain a generous policy towards those wishing to come here."[46]

CHAPTER 7

THE ONLY MIDDLE THERE IS

Grant us, O Lord, the understanding to work together, across all the
boundaries of nation, culture, and creed, so that we may truly unite
the world in hope rather than separate men by an abyss of fear.
—Theodore M. Hesburgh, CSC
National Academy of Sciences Invocation, 1963

Óscar Romero's appointment as archbishop of San Salvador on
February 3, 1977, was as predictable as his assassination on March
24, 1980. Born on August 15, 1917, in Ciudad Barrios, Romero began
studying for the priesthood in his native El Salvador but was sent to
the Gregorian University in Rome to complete his studies amid the
tumult of World War II. After returning home in 1943, Romero served
for more than twenty years as a parish priest. He was then appointed as
secretary to El Salvador's Council of Bishops in 1966 and editor of the
newspaper for the archdiocese, *Orientación*, in 1971.

Romero's editorial predecessor, Father Rutilio Sánchez, "aroused
controversy by focusing on El Salvador's social questions. When
Sánchez went so far as to praise the Columbian guerilla priest, Camillo
Torres, Archbishop [Luis] Chávez removed him."[1] El Salvador, like
several of its neighbors, was the subject of rising tensions and even violence between, in El Salvador's case, wealthy landowners and peasant

farmers or campesinos. Many within the Church became advocates of liberation theology—a theological school of thought rooted in God's preference for the poor and, at times, intermixed with Marxist political thought. Under Romero, however, readers of *Orientación* noticed a quick shift toward "less controversial topics like drugs, alcoholism, and pornography, and to more cautious views of social questions, when they were mentioned."[2]

Romero was appointed an auxiliary bishop for the Archdiocese of San Salvador in 1970, bishop of the Diocese of Santiago de Maria in 1974, and then archbishop in 1977. Joseph B. Frazier, an Associated Press correspondent in El Salvador from 1979 to 1986, noted that "the Roman Catholic Church in El Salvador was (and generally remains) fairly conservative, and military governments had long tried to influence the country's top cleric." At the time of his appointment, Romero "looked and acted like the last person in the world who would be a burr in the blanket of the military or aristocracy."[3] Romero biographer James R. Brockman offered that to individuals who pondered how the Church could support the poor, "Romero seemed still wedded to the old ways and his ostentatious ordination an offense to the many who still lived in dire poverty in El Salvador."[4]

Shortly after his appointment as archbishop, a Jesuit priest and friend of Romero's, Father Rutilio Grande, was killed "as he headed toward a church north of the capital in the Aguilares area to celebrate Mass." Grande was a proponent of liberation theology, and "many who knew Romero said the Rutilio Grande murder radicalized him."[5] If nothing else, one could argue Grande's murder compelled Romero to recognize that even the Church was not immune to the lengths the military and aristocracy would go to prevent reform.

Romero never became a supporter of liberation theology, but he clearly aligned himself with the message of Paul VI's encyclical *Evangelii Nuntiandi* (On Evangelization in the Modern World), in which the pope opened by recognizing that people in many parts of the world "are buoyed up by hope but at the same time often oppressed by fear and distress." Romero became one who recognized fear and oppression but refused to disconnect it from Paul VI's contention that "there is no doubt that the effort to proclaim the Gospel to the people of today… is a service rendered to the Christian community and also to the whole of humanity" (*Evangelii Nuntiandi* 1).[6] The poor and oppressed were worthy of the Church's support, but the ones who oppressed the poor were in their own ways worthy of its support, too.

Archbishop Romero's weekly radio homilies would become among the most popular in El Salvador. After months of growing violence, Romero brought the ramifications of *Evangelii Nuntiandi* to bear in his homily on March 23, 1980, when he addressed members of El Salvador's army:

> Brothers, you are part of our own people. You are killing your own brother and sister campesinos, and against any order a man may give to kill, God's law must prevail, "You shall not kill!" (Exodus 20:13). No soldier is obliged to obey an order against the law of God. No one has to observe an immoral law. It is time now for you to reclaim your conscience and to obey your conscience rather than the command to sin….In the name of God, then, in the name of this suffering people whose laments rise up each day more tumultuously toward heaven, I beg you, I beseech you, I order you in the name of God: stop the repression![7]

While celebrating Mass the following day in the chapel at San Salvador's Hospital de la Divina Providencia, Romero was murdered by a gunman who was never apprehended for his crime.

On November 24, 1987, the *New York Times* reported El Salvador's then president, José Napoleón Duarte, a 1948 graduate of the University of Notre Dame and former student of Father Hesburgh, "said a close military associate of Mr. [Roberto] d'Aubuisson helped plan and direct the killing of the Archbishop. Mr. Duarte contended that the associate, Capt. Alvaro Rafael Saravia, then visited Mr. d'Aubuisson to confirm that the assassination had been carried out."[8] D'Aubuisson was an adversary, politically to the right of Duarte.

Duarte and his family had also been victims of violence. Beginning in 1964, he had served three terms as mayor of San Salvador. According to Russell Crandall, author of *The Salvador Option*, Duarte's "protests against the military regime in the aftermath of the stolen 1972 elections led to his arrest at the National Police headquarters, where he suffered a smashed cheekbone, a black eye, and charges of treason." Crandall noted that "international pressure, including from Notre Dame president Reverend Theodore Hesburgh ... helped ensure Duarte's exile to Venezuela."[9]

The years following Romero's 1980 murder saw intense civil war. Even so, in 1984 El Salvador elected its first civilian president since 1931 when Duarte defeated d'Aubuisson. Two years earlier, in elections for seats in the National Congress, Duarte's Christian Democratic Party secured twenty-four seats, d'Aubuisson's Nationalist Republican Alliance (ARENA) secured nineteen seats, and the National Conciliation Party secured fourteen seats. At the time, Hesburgh acknowledged, "I think there is a limit to what he [Duarte] can do. He can't control his right and he can't control the left. He's in the middle but he's the only middle there is."[10]

As members of a nine-person team of observers of the 1982 elections, Representative John Murtha (D-Pennsylvania) and Hesburgh "rode aboard a Salvadoran air force UH1-H 'Huey' helicopter to check polling places." They made "a full-day helicopter tour ... of provinces with the heaviest guerrilla activity and questioned voters about the large turnout."[11]

In the end, they found "thousands of Salvadorans have walked miles to the polls, always within the sound and danger of small-arms fire." At one site they visited, a funeral procession emerged from the trees. A mother was burying her son who had been shot at a polling place; no priest was available to officiate. The *Los Angeles Times* said, "Hesburgh consoled the mother and performed simple rites for the victim in Spanish." Hesburgh reported, "I gave him a blessing and said the prayers of burial, and gave her a rosary I had gotten from the Pope."[12]

Even amid the violence, Salvadorans were on the path to fair elections and the much longer path to peace.

As the Church's public intellectual, Hesburgh viewed his mediating role in international relations as one by which peace was forged between both individuals and nations. Eternity was defined by the peaceable relations found in ongoing fellowship with God. Due to human depravity and the ways it manifested itself this side of eternity, faith in Christ compelled people to do what they could to broker peace between neighbors, ranging from individuals to nations. Such efforts were possible because of the incarnation of Christ and the ongoing presence of the Holy Spirit.

As a result, Hesburgh often referred to Christmas as the point in time when the peace of God interrupted the world and the strife that all too often defined it. For example, in "The Catholic Spirit of Christmas," he argued, "For the Catholic, all history revolves around that event which is central in liturgy as it is in life. Christmas is the birthday of an era, the inauguration of a culture, the beginning of a creed, the fountainhead of man's hope." On that day, Christ came "as a sharer of our nature and our lot." As a result, Christ fully participated in all our struggles. However, "the Catholic spirit of Christmas, to its last fiber, is dyed in divinity." Christ was not only fully human but was also fully divine. He thus came not only to participate in our struggles but also to share with all "that God has come to redeem His people."[13]

Beyond the Holy Family, perhaps the only people who initially appreciated the significance of that day were those to whom the angels appeared—not people resting in palaces but keeping watch over sheep in the fields. As he did in a couple of other related writings, Hesburgh recounted that "it is only by recalling the birth of Our Lord that we take renewed courage to sing: 'Glory to God in the highest; and on earth peace to men of good will.'"[14] With shepherds in the fields, the announcement was made that a new era had begun—an era not defined by strife and force but peace and reconciliation.

ATOMS FOR PEACE

Hesburgh believed and acted upon his conviction that peaceful relations among nations began with peaceful relations between individuals. Although that conviction was rooted in the incarnation, the presence of nuclear weapons also motivated Hesburgh until the very end of his life to work for peace. As mentioned in chapter 2, looming in the back of his mind concerning the need for a clear and defining purpose for the development of science and technology was the possible misuse of nuclear energy.

With that impending threat, in 1956 the United Nations labored to establish what came to be known as the International Atomic Energy Agency (IAEA) or Atoms for Peace. Pope Pius XII deferred to New York's Cardinal Francis Spellman to make the delegate appointments. Hesburgh turned down a request from Spellman the prior year to have Notre Dame's football team play the University of Maryland in a bowl game, the proceeds of which would go to an orphanage. Although such a decision was premised on a policy Hesburgh had set to keep athletes from playing in such events during finals, he believed he owed Spellman a favor.

As with almost all of the other appointments Hesburgh accepted over the course of his lifetime, Spellman "assured me that it would not take that much of my time because even though the conference was scheduled for seven weeks, I would not have to be there [at the United Nations] the entire time."[15] Little did Hesburgh know in 1956, his appointment as the Vatican's delegate to the IAEA would continue until 1970.

Fortunately for Hesburgh, the Vatican had two delegates, the second, upon Hesburgh's recommendation, was initially Marston Morse, a mathematician who held an appointment at the Institute for Advanced Study. In addition, the Vatican granted Morse and Hesburgh "full power to discuss, approve, and sign any document of the conference in the name of the Vatican without prior instructions."[16] When

Morse resigned a year later, Hesburgh "suggested Frank Folsom, the recently retired president of the Radio Corporation of America"[17] who served until Folsom passed away in 1970.

When offering the sermon at Folsom's funeral on January 16 of that year, Hesburgh said,

> No one will ever know how the power of faith and hope and love mediated peace during a precarious and difficult period of history, and how much the more hopeful signs of today result quite directly from those efforts in darker days. But his faith begot faith, his hope engendered hope, and his very real love attracted those without much faith or hope that endeared them to what he stood for.[18]

Hesburgh believed he, Folsom, and the IAEA "made some very important strides on behalf of humanity." For example, they "helped many Third World countries make use of radioisotopes in agriculture, in medicine, and in other ways that improved their standards of living." In addition, they "laid the groundwork for the landmark Nuclear Proliferation Treaty that we eventually produced and more than one hundred nations signed."[19]

As echoed in the sermon at Folsom's funeral, the groundwork that made those efforts possible came through the establishment of human relations between people previously socialized not to trust one another, as was the case with the Soviets and the Americans. Early on in his work, Hesburgh believed he "could do a better job as a delegate if I could establish a personal relationship with at least one of the Russians at the conference." In particular, the relationship he forged with Vasily Emelyanov, at the time a "university professor, metallurgist, and a corresponding member of the National Academy of Sciences in the Soviet Union" yielded dividends on professional and personal levels.[20]

Part of Folsom's commitment to the IAEA came because he was a grandfather; he wanted his grandchildren to live in a world free of the fear of a nuclear holocaust. After realizing he was not the only grandfather with the IAEA, "Folsom started something called the International Grandfathers Club. He named himself president and appointed Emelyanov as his vice president." Such efforts brought Emelyanov to contend that the delegates from the Vatican "were his friends ... that we always told the truth, [and] we were always ready to work for peace."[21]

THE PEACE OF GOD

Peace between individuals and nations was a theme Hesburgh addressed in his public remarks even before assuming the presidency at Notre Dame. In March 1951, for example, Hesburgh offered an address at the University of North Carolina-Chapel Hill titled "The Peace of God" in which he began by acknowledging, "People all over the world yearn today for peace, and yet, feel deeply frustrated at their inability to do anything about achieving it on a world wide scale."[22] Although some individuals find themselves called to contribute to brokering peace on such a scale, such efforts are predicated upon a myriad of individual efforts.

Those efforts, according to Hesburgh, "can be achieved by any person willing to try." To reinforce the significance of those efforts, Hesburgh asked his audience whether they ever stopped "to think that the tensions and conflicts throughout the world today are little more than a vast mirroring of the tensions and conflicts that tear the souls of individual human beings like ourselves." As a result, "If people are generally at peace, certainly the world would be at peace."[23]

When trying to define peace, however, Hesburgh acknowledged that his own "words fail." He turned to Saint Thomas Aquinas's definition of peace, one that applies to individual persons or nations: "in three words—he called it the 'tranquility of order.'"[24] Hesburgh referred once again to the incarnation after reviewing more secular assessments of Saint Thomas's words. In particular, he said, "Most of you must recall the divinely inspired song of the angel the night Christ Our Lord was born—'Glory to God in the highest, and on earth peace to men of good will. 'Here is a formula for peace that will really work if we fully understand it."[25] On Christmas Day, the disorder of the world once again began to be properly ordered.

To participate in the peace Christ made possible, Hesburgh asked his audience to commit themselves to the truth of three theological propositions about the proper order of the world:

> Grant that God created everything to glorify the beauty, the goodness, the truth that God *is* and always has been and always will be. Grant that God established a basic order in the world, since many have argued from the reality of this striking order to the fact of God's existence. Grant that there is glory given to God in the highest by the order and beauty of the created universe.[26]

Human beings "alone can consciously earn and enjoy the peace of God, and on the other hand, man alone can consciously reject God and His peace that results from keeping all things in order."[27]

Hesburgh was eager to share this message concerning the peace of God and the "tranquility of order" with any number of audiences. In November 1953, for example, he delivered a sermon for the Catholic Lawyers Guild at their meeting in Chicago. As his text, he took Apostle Paul's words to the Galatians (2:20), "'I live, now not I, but Christ liveth in me.'"[28] Hesburgh opened by noting "the life of every saint is a kind of continuing Incarnation of Christ, so that Christ is permitted to live again on earth and to manifest His saving grace in every walk of life."[29] Attorneys were called, he said, to be an active presence in the world, to be Christ, and to bring order out of disorder.

As an example, Hesburgh turned to Saint Thomas More who, after considering the contemplative life of a monk, chose the active life of "marriage, family, and professional life."[30] King Henry VIII's desire for the dissolution of his marriage to Catherine of Aragon compelled More "to decide with the king or with Christ."[31] More chose Christ. Hesburgh implored his audience to take up More's example "for the rearing of Christian families, for order in the legislative process, for the maintenance of true liberty against all that would unjustly hinder it, [and] for the promotion of peace on earth, at home and abroad."[32]

Four years later, Hesburgh shared a comparable message with Air Force staff chaplains in Washington, DC. Compelled at times to "decide with king or with Christ," chaplains, as with attorneys, often found themselves bringing order out of disorder. At that time, the disorder on most minds was the one caused by the tensions between the nuclear superpowers in the United States and the Soviet Union. However, Hesburgh opened by acknowledging, "The heart of the conflict is beyond the physical forces of manpower, strategic bases, and nuclear weapons." What was truly at stake was "the significant clash of diametrically opposed ideas and beliefs."[33] The ideas and beliefs that separated the Soviet Union and the United States at that time respectively upheld a view that all that existed was a material reality versus a material reality defined and shaped by a spiritual reality. Strategic bases and nuclear weapons posed real threats, but they were symptoms of an illness that plagued not only the Soviet Union but also the United States.

Hesburgh said, "We are not merely interested in defeating Communism as an opposing world view. We are rather seeking for the dynamic sources of life in our own democratic form." The reality, as Hesburgh saw it, was that "if Communism were to be wiped from the face of the earth today or tomorrow, we would not ourselves be better than we are today, only perhaps less harassed." As a result, "the most effective kind of death blow to Communism and its claims" would come through an urgent assessment of "those truths by which we profess to live."[34] The disorder that separated the Soviets and the Americans was real and based on at least two levels of claims. However, the warning Hesburgh sought to issue on that day—concerning the more fundamental level of strife Americans faced—involved their inability to live by the truths they professed.

As a corrective, Hesburgh reminded the chaplains gathered that "religious faith has inspired and directed man in all of his noble institutions, since faith allows us to see man in the totality of his being and nature, as it were, with the eyes of God."[35] By now, one is not likely surprised to read that Hesburgh claimed Christian anthropology as a fundamental component of properly ordered relations. Humans, when left to their depravity, run the risk of objectifying one another (and perhaps even themselves) and, in turn, viewing one another as merely physical beings. At their root, disordered relations come as a result of not understanding people in their totality. What, then, does it mean to appreciate others as physical beings, intellectual beings, and emotional beings, and, in the end, what defines and unifies such forms of understanding—that is, spiritual beings?

That spiritual corrective was rooted in an understanding "that there is one supreme, personal God." That understanding, in turn, put one's understanding of humanity, "our faith in man," in proper order. Hesburgh thus believed that such a person was "not the self-sufficient man of [Jean-Jacques] Rousseau and the naturalists, but a man who possesses dignity and immortality because God has created him after His own image and likeness." Humans are not worthy of that dignity because of their physical presence or even their intelligence. They are worthy of that dignity and are called to live in properly ordered relations with one another because "God has created [them] after His own image and likeness."[36]

Hesburgh then argued, "It is faith in this total view of man that gives depth and substance and vitality to the democratic charter, and it is in this sense that religious faith is necessary for a living democracy."[37] At this point, Hesburgh cited Jacques Maritain at length and the assertions Maritain made in *Christianity and Democracy*. For Maritain, humanity must

> keep faith in the forward march of humanity despite all of the temptations to despair of man that are furnished by history and particularly contemporary society…to have faith in liberty and fraternity, an heroic inspiration and an heroic belief are needed which fortify and vivify reason, and which

none other than Jesus of Nazareth brought forth in the world.[38]

Only then, according to Hesburgh, could the disorder plaguing Americans be resolved. Such a level of disorder, regardless of what stood between the Soviets and Americans, was more fundamental and thus necessary to efforts being made for "liberty and fraternity" among all people.

Finally, Hesburgh was invited to share this message through an invocation he offered in Washington, DC, before members of the National Academy of Sciences in 1963. On that day, Hesburgh prayed before his gathered audience

> that science might become in our day the great liberator, a force for peace in the hands of the scientists, not a scourge for mankind, a demonic power....Grant us the wisdom, O Lord, so to dominate ourselves that we may be liberators and not destroyers, creating harbingers of hope not specters of the ultimate destruction.[39]

As was always the case for Hesburgh, the concern over the misuse of nuclear energy was on his mind. However, how people understood themselves and, in turn, the relations they were called to have with one another was fundamental to properly ordered relations between individuals and even nations.

THE PRESENCE OF GOD

If one was not surprised that a Christian anthropology was a critical component of Hesburgh's understanding of properly ordered relations between individuals and nations, one is probably not surprised now to consider another critical component: Hesburgh's understanding of God's presence being woven into human interdependence. During the 1970s, optimism surfaced that humanity was "entering a time when there is less chance of a cataclysmic nuclear war—mankind's final war." In Hesburgh's estimation, the threat of a nuclear holocaust compelled allies and adversaries alike among "the great developed countries of the world" to "pay little attention to the needs, the interests, the wishes, and the humanity of the vast bulk of mankind: the fully two and a half billion people who live in countries we call 'poor.'"[40]

Six months after the Cuban Missile Crisis took the world to the brink of nuclear war, John XXIII issued the encyclical *Pacem in Terris*. Eleven years later and during that time of optimism, Hesburgh addressed a gathering in Washington, DC, seeking to unpack the full ramifications of that encyclical. Hesburgh viewed that event as an apt moment to review "the issue of equity among nations on planet earth." As he had done in relation to other topics, Hesburgh argued, "Today, we in the United States are the heirs of a bountiful heritage, both in material wealth and in the character of our people. Yet in our amassing of physical abundance, we are now creating problems for the rest of the world—and for our own future." Hesburgh acknowledged, "Now we know the supply [of natural resources] is not inexhaustible, nor are we only depleting only those resources within our own borders." Peace in our time demanded not only a resolve to use nuclear energy properly but to understand how "isolated lives of abundance would be mocked by indifference to the needs and desires of the vast majority of the human family."[41] Peace could not hold in a world with such a disordered division of resources.

In October 1973, Hesburgh lobbied a comparable theme in Washington, DC, this time at the International Development Conference. With this group, Hesburgh took a more pragmatic approach and argued that a variety of "systems were designed by the rich countries to meet rich country needs." For example, when it came to trade and monetary systems, to name only two, Hesburgh contended rich countries did not intend to "discriminate against the poor countries. For the most part, they simply did not think of these countries and their needs."[42] Hesburgh cited the practice of countervailing in terms of trade systems and open seas as an example that favors wealthy nations at the expense of less wealthy nations. The interdependent nature of the world now brought forward an understanding that such a disordered array of systems was not conducive to peaceable relations between people and nations.

To bring order out of this sense of disorder, Hesburgh also proposed "a bias favoring the poor," but doing so, as mentioned earlier, was rooted in Hesburgh's belief in the interdependent nature of humanity. He also argued that realism would lead a person to the wisdom of what he proposed. In particular, he argued, "It is in our self-interest for nations to attend to the international economic, social, and political health of our planet today, just as surely as it is in the interest of the people of any local community to accept restraints on individuals for the common good of the whole community." Such disorder is not sustainable. "The goods of this world were not created for the over-consumption of one-fifth of its people while the other four-fifths starve."[43]

Finally, Hesburgh wove a comparable iteration of this theme concerning God's presence and human interdependence in an address at the Bicentennial Conference on Religious Liberty in Philadelphia in April 1976. Hesburgh spent the majority of that address drawing out how "religious liberty was established in America by disestablishment" and tracing "the enlargement of human dignity and rights in America."[44] When concluding his address, Hesburgh turned to the work of Maritain and observations Maritain offered in *Reflections on America*. Maritain and his wife, Raïssa, fled France during World War II. In the United States, Maritain claimed he found an "astounding adventure: it is the value and dignity of the common man, the value and dignity of the people."[45]

Hesburgh contended, however, that properly ordered relations between people and nations mean that "the adventure must now be worldwide." What was initiated in the United States "will not really be successful unless human dignity and human rights are vindicated worldwide, for all humans have this God-given dignity and deserve these inalienable rights, be they religious or civil or, most fundamentally, just human."[46] As a result, Hesburgh believed the bicentennial was an apt time to "back, as a nation, a new national Declaration, this time not for Independence, but for Interdependence."[47]

THE NUCLEAR THREAT (REVISITED)

Unfortunately, the time when "there [was] less chance of a cataclysmic nuclear war—mankind's final war" passed as the world witnessed a renewal of an arms race between nuclear superpowers during the 1980s. As a result, on Wednesday, November 11, 1981, about 250 universities across the United States agreed to host symposia on peace in the nuclear age. As part of their efforts, Notre Dame hosted a lecture by James E. Muller, a cardiologist who served on the faculty at Harvard University Medical School and was cofounder of International Physicians for the Prevention of Nuclear War, an organization that won the Nobel Peace Prize in 1985. According to Hesburgh, Muller offered a "graphic lecture on what would happen if a one megaton nuclear bomb were detonated over the adjoining city of South Bend."[48]

When walking back to his office that evening, Hesburgh realized that "this great University and all the other problems that had preoccupied my time would be totally irrelevant: no people, no problems." He decided "then and there it seemed important to disengage myself from these other concerns, except education, and to do whatever I might about this quintessential threat of nuclear annihilation."[49] Many of the speeches Hesburgh gave over the course of the mid- to late 1980s—before the National Academy of Education,[50] at the University of California–San Diego,[51] before the Bulletin of the Atomic Scientists,[52] and before the Carnegie Council for Ethics and International Affairs[53]—focused on the threat posed by nuclear war, the United States Catholic Bishops' Pastoral Letter on War and Peace, and meetings convened by the Pontifical Academy of Sciences.

In response to the renewal of the arms race between the United States and the Soviet Union, the National Conference of Catholic Bishops issued a pastoral letter on May 3, 1983, titled "The Challenge of Peace: God's Promise and Our Response." Later that year, Father Philip J. Murnion, founder of the National Pastoral Life Center, published *Catholics and Nuclear War*, a volume that included the full text of the letter, responses by various scholars, and a foreword by Hesburgh. In that foreword, Hesburgh noted the threat of nuclear war constituted a previously unseen moral problem. Never before had humanity possessed the ability in so little time to destroy itself so many times over. After applying the theological insights afforded by the pacifist and just war traditions, Hesburgh noted the bishops concluded that the "initiation of nuclear war at any level cannot be morally justified in any perceivable situation."[54]

On a more personal level, Hesburgh was involved in a series of meetings convened by the Pontifical Academy of Sciences in the early 1980s. He highly valued the venue that brought leading scientists and theologians together to focus on the common challenge of nuclear war. The group concluded its work by issuing an appeal to national leaders, scientists, religious leaders, and people everywhere to draw on their respective expertise and do what they could, as in the case of people everywhere, "to reaffirm their faith in the destiny of humanity, to insist that the avoidance of war is a common responsibility, to combat the belief that nuclear war is unavoidable, and to labor unceasingly toward insuring the future of generations to come."[55]

Toward the end of his foreword, Hesburgh argued, "This is not a Soviet or an American problem. It is a human problem. We may continue creation or utterly destroy it. What sin could be greater? To reverse creation must be the worst blasphemy imaginable."[56]

◊ ◊ ◊

On Sunday, May 19, 1985, José Napoleón Duarte returned to Notre Dame to offer the university's commencement address and receive an honorary doctorate. Outside the commencement venue, "about 300 demonstrators representing Marxist-Leninist, socialist and religious organizations in the Midwest waved banners and chanted in support of the Salvadoran insurgents and against United States policies in Central America. They called Mr. Duarte a 'front for the death squads.'" Inside, graduates would hear Duarte turn from recollections of his days as a student to reflections on his calling to lead El Salvador. "'It was my most intimate conviction,' Duarte said, 'that my obligation lay in freeing my country from the two totalitarian extremes: the Marxists and the Fascists.'"[57]

Due to that commitment, Duarte and his family suffered more violence. Less than four months later, Duarte's daughter, Inés Guadalupe Duarte Durán and her friend, Ana Cecilia Villeda, were kidnapped in San Salvador on September 10, 1985. They were released on October 25, 1985, but, in exchange, "The Government said it released 22 political prisoners and provided safe passage for 96 guerrillas disabled in the war."[58]

Duarte left office in 1989 and died a year later. Salvadorans still face many miles on the long path to peace. In terms of Duarte's accusations concerning the identity of Óscar Romero's assassin, "A United Nations–backed 'Truth Commission' investigation, published in 1993, concluded that the mastermind of the assassination was Roberto d'Aubuisson."[59]

On October 14, 2018, Pope Francis canonized Romero as a saint. Time will tell, however, how history will remember Duarte. Writing in the preface to Duarte's autobiography, Hesburgh offered,

> The only way to avoid criticism is to sit on the fence and do nothing, except maybe to criticize others who are trying to create a better and more just world. I have received dozens of letters from critics who wrote them safely from comfortable quarters far from the fray. I am sure President Duarte has received many more, because he has been sitting, by his choice, in the middle of the target, the most critical spot of all.[60]

CONCLUSION
CHRIST ALONE MEDIATES PERFECTLY

This function of mediation looks both to God and to men: to God in worship and atonement for sin, the basis of disunity, and to men in order to bring them divine grace and truth in Christ, the center of unity.

—Theodore M. Hesburgh, CSC
The Theology of Catholic Action, *1946*

The Federal Bureau of Investigation's (FBI) file for Father Theodore Martin Hesburgh is approximately 450 pages in length. Most of its content is from background checks conducted prior to the offer of a government appointment or the granting of a security clearance. Whatever the purpose, the contents of Hesburgh's file make for rather mundane reading.

For example, in a letter dated February 15, 1962, the FBI's director, J. Edgar Hoover, confirmed to Secretary of State Dean Rusk, that Hesburgh was "a loyal American of excellent character, reputation and associates."[1]

In a letter dated November 18, 1974, the FBI's Clarence H. Kelley confirmed to Jane Dannenhauer, staff assistant for security with the White House, that information has been received from the United States Secret Service; Office of Security, Department of State; Office of Security, Department of Health, Education, and Welfare; Naval Investigative Service, Naval Intelligence Command; and [NAME REDACTED] indicating their files contain either no record or no additional pertinent information concerning Father Hesburgh.[2]

In a report filed on June 13, 1991, FBI agents noted the South Bend (Indiana) Police Department and the St. Joseph's County Sheriff's Department "advised they had no arrest record for appointee [Hesburgh]." In addition, "the files of the INDIANA STATE POLICE were checked through the Indiana Data and Communications System (IDACS) and revealed no identifiable information regarding appointee."[3]

The same report noted, "Last year he met with the Presidents of Brazil and Chile. In January 1991, he met with [Mikhail] Gorbachev [President of the Soviet Union] as a member of the International Foundation for the Development and Survival of Humankind. All of his meetings with foreign officials are for business reasons." Repeatedly, reports such as the one dated June 13, 1991, noted, "Appointee is loyal to the United States," and "He has not used illegal drugs and does not abuse prescription medicine."[4]

Perhaps the most interesting details included in the 450 pages of documentation concerned Hesburgh's finances and the individuals with whom he associated. In relation to his personal finances, it seemed agents did not quite know what to make of the religious order's vow of poverty. In relation to questions about his associates, agents seemed baffled, describing the relatively barren room Hesburgh occupied in Corby Hall, the rectory on Notre Dame's campus that served as a residence for approximately forty Congregation of Holy Cross priests. Although the scope of the inquiries was understandably limited to matters that would prohibit the granting of an appointment or security clearance, little to no details exist concerning what animated Hesburgh and, in particular, why he was willing to serve in the requested capacities. Very few U.S. citizens—or members of the Church—have served in such a diverse array of roles. As a result, Hesburgh's record of service, while imperfect, is historically significant. But here and now, a specific aspect of his service must be considered—what animated him to fulfill his calling as the Church's public intellectual?

SACRAMENTAL CHARACTER

As previously noted, Hesburgh's understanding of his identity was rooted in his belief in the sacramental character of life and the ways all members of Christ's body were called to use their diverse array of gifts and talents. Hesburgh did so as a priest and member of the Congregation of Holy Cross who was given considerable intellectual gifts and required as few as four hours of sleep a night. However, as far back as his dissertation and first book, *The Theology of Catholic Action*, Hesburgh contended, perhaps in anticipation of Vatican II, that clergy and laity alike were called to do God's work. He may have fulfilled his calling as a priest and as a mediator of God's grace via his administration of the sacraments, but laypeople were also called to fulfill their own callings as participants in the sacramental character Christ made possible.

In *The Theology of Catholic Action*, for example, Hesburgh argued, "The layman's participation in the apostolic work of Christ can only be fully understood in terms of that objective work of Christ to which it is wholly ordained." The context behind Hesburgh's reference to the objective work of Christ is the belief posed by heretical groups that Christ's ministry "was only an inspiring example to be followed." Hesburgh believed Christ offered "an inspiring example to be followed"—and also so much more; the grace Christ made possible through the historical event of the incarnation and present in the sacraments made it possible for all members of the Church to be participants in "Christ's mediatorial activity."[5] In the end, Christ's example alone, however noteworthy, would prove to be an insufficient means for salvation.

That example, however, was also defined by Christ's larger mediatorial activity in which all persons could now participate.

By now, one is not surprised that Hesburgh turned to Saint Thomas Aquinas for his understanding of Christ's example and its larger mediatorial context. Saint Thomas made no distinction between clergy and the laity when addressing "whether the sacramental character is the character of Christ?" Saint Thomas also noted, "A character is properly a kind of seal, whereby something is marked, as being ordained to some particular end." In his estimation (and Hesburgh's), that end was twofold. First, the faithful are "principally [deputed or assigned] to the enjoyment of glory. And for this purpose they are marked by the seal of grace." Second, Saint Thomas contended, "Each of the faithful is deputed to receive, or to bestow upon others, things pertaining to the worship of God."[6]

As previously noted, the manner in which Hesburgh was called to bestow upon others "things pertaining to the worship of God" came in ways he would not have previously anticipated. When the Eisenhower administration asked him to serve on the National Science Board, his first inclination was to admit he was trained in theology and philosophy, not science. When the Carter administration asked him to lead the Select Commission on Immigration and Refugee Policy, he initially claimed he knew little about the complexities of immigration. Hesburgh's education in philosophy and theology taught him how to learn and structure knowledge. Celebrating Mass daily renewed his calling to bestow upon others "things pertaining to the worship of God," which could range from the proper use of nuclear energy to the proper receipt of displaced persons.

As a result, a proper understanding of things pertaining to the worship of God that mediation often demands may involve redemption. A power such as nuclear energy could be used for destructive means previously unimagined by humanity, or it could be used for peaceful means. The admittance of displaced persons could possibly subject them to further oppression and/or the oppression of others, or it could be offered in ways that grant aid and comfort to as many people as possible. Christ's "priestly mediation is continued, participated variously by all His members, who through His life-giving sacraments partake of the influence of the greatest sacrament of all: His sacred Humanity, 'the source of all priesthood.'" In ways never estimated, members of Christ's body are called to serve as living bridges "between God and men."[7]

IMPERFECT PARTICIPATION

Hesburgh believed that despite "being ordained to some particular end," members of Christ's body remain incomplete participants in the calling to serve as living bridges between "God and men." The integrity of grace is not dependent on human efforts but on God as made possible and exemplified in the integrity of Christ's sacrifice. Hesburgh did not intend for such an assertion to minimize the impact human beings can have when they submit to their varied callings to serve as mediators between God and humanity. If anything, his conviction, drawn again from Saint Thomas, was intended to place the power of God and members of God's creation in proper perspective.

Hesburgh supported that perspective via four interrelated assertions. First, "Since Christ is [the] unique, and universal Head of mankind, His priesthood is unique and universal."[8] In Hesburgh's estimation, Christ alone was worthy of the sacrifice offered on Calvary on which the integrity of all other sacraments is dependent. As Saint Thomas noted, "The priesthood of Christ has full power to expiate sins."[9] Again, Christ was not merely an example worth following; the unique character of his priesthood is evident in the ways it makes possible all other forms of that priesthood, however imperfect they may be this side of eternity. His priesthood was not only unique but universal. As a result, it did not apply to a select few or even a chosen people but now to all who profess faith in Christ. Regardless of how human beings may draw lines between one another, Christ's priesthood was made available to all people.

Second, Hesburgh argued that "since his [Christ's] action as Priest includes the full scope of His apostolic power to teach, govern, and sanctify, all participation in His priestly power must be considered in terms of these powers which he conferred upon his Church for the continuation of his priestly mission."[10] Admittedly risking oversimplification of what Hesburgh noted, individuals who participate in Christ's mediatorial priesthood are called to exercise that calling in ways both within and beyond the Church. As echoed in the introduction above, modern society often seeks to quarantine faith as private experience. However, here Hesburgh argued that regardless of the context, whether it be exercised via acts of teaching, governing, or sanctification, Christ's mediatorial calling is relevant and necessary. Christ "alone mediates perfectly,"[11] but the range of contexts in which that mediation is needed is as wide as the expanse of God's creation.

Third, Hesburgh contended, "Since His [Christ's] priestly power is derived from the fact of his Incarnation, the effects of his priesthood perdure forever."[12] Echoing Saint Thomas, the term *perdure* in Hesburgh's usage represents that Christ's priestly power remains in existence and does so forever. As a result, that power did not merely exist at a particular time but exists forever or until the consummation of time at Christ's return. Saint Thomas made this claim when noting that "the end of the sacrifice which Christ offered consisted not in temporal but in eternal good."[13] However imperfect they may be, Christ's followers, regardless of the age in which they live, are granted access to that sacrifice. The challenge for those followers is prayerfully to seek God's wisdom in order to discern how that sacrifice is to be mediated in relation to the challenges they face.

Finally, Hesburgh contended, "Others may cooperate in His perfect mediatorial work of uniting men to God, but as St. Thomas teaches, they will do so only '*dispositive et ministerialiter*.'"[14] Regardless of where or when members of Christ's body live, they are called to be adaptable in how they minister. This does not mean they need to adapt the end they are called to serve, yet where and when one lives will demand one adapt to achieve that end. Christ "alone mediates perfectly," yet all who are members of his body are called to mediate between the hopes of heaven and the realities of earth whenever and wherever they live.

Again, Hesburgh likely never envisioned components of his calling would involve him in deep discussions about science and technology or immigration. In addition, as shown in what he wrote decades before receiving those calls, he knew that his efforts to mediate between the hopes of heaven and the realities of earth would be imperfect. Regardless, for reasons shrouded in God's infinite wisdom, he was called by public officials and had to formulate answers.

FIRM IN HOPE

The difference between what one perceives as possible and impossible is ultimately rooted in the virtue of hope. In contrast to popular perceptions, hope is not wishful thinking. Hope is marked by a sacramental character and ordained to a particular end—an end ultimately defined by the worship of God. The reality in which hope is rooted is the incarnation.

As a result, Hesburgh committed himself to saying Mass daily. On most days, he celebrated Mass at Notre Dame. His travels and his commitments also led him to celebrate Mass in places ranging from Washington, DC, to Moscow and Tehran to Jerusalem. Geographically, no details exist concerning the farthest north Hesburgh ever said Mass. However, in 1963 he celebrated Mass at the South Pole while traveling with the National Science Board.

For Hesburgh, hope was thus an understanding of the present and future that was rooted in a particular event in the past. Christ's sacrifice made realities of life's triumph over death and good's triumph over evil. This side of eternity, human depravity would continue to rear its head. No easy answers exist as Christ "alone mediates perfectly." By virtue of the grace made possible by Christ's sacrifice, however, others who called to mediate in Christ's name could do so rooted in an understanding of what the incarnation made possible. No longer were the hopes of heaven inaccessible to the realities of earth. Human beings could prayerfully discern how properly to use nuclear energy and properly welcome displaced persons. Mass destruction or ceaseless oppression was not all that awaited humanity.

For Hesburgh, hope rooted in the incarnation and reenacted in the Mass compelled him to believe that the eternal truths of theology and philosophy were applicable to any challenge plaguing humanity both now and in the future. He realized that knowledge, especially as organized by the modern university, was defined by isolated disciplines. Without a doubt, benefits come to scholars who mine the depths of those disciplines in specialized ways. But when scholars were called upon to address a particular challenge plaguing humanity, no one discipline could have all the answers. Nor, it seemed, could anyone link together what they collectively offered in a useful way.

Hesburgh believed this challenge plagued the modern university because it failed to appreciate what theology and, when disconnected from theology, philosophy properly offered. As previously noted, the modern university viewed theology at best as the language learned by the practice of a privatized faith. Philosophy was then just another discipline practiced by scholars who spoke jargon only they understood. In contrast, Hesburgh believed that when theology was the language learned by the practice of a faith rooted in the incarnation, the disciplines could begin to find their full meaning and use to a world desperately in need of what they could offer.

Only then (to return to these examples), could one fully explore questions concerning the proper use of nuclear energy as critical not only to human survival but also to human flourishing. Only then could one fully explore why the proper admittance of displaced persons was critical to human survival and human flourishing. The answers depended on lessons offered by a host of disciplines—as they were coherently linked to the realities of earth with the hopes of heaven. As noted in chapter 2 and drawn from the speech delivered at Saint Mary's College in honor of the opening of its science building, Hesburgh contended,

Now is the day when we must face the herculean intellectual task of achieving the unity of knowledge that will recognize all that is validly known today, and all of the valid ways of knowing. We have had enough of philosophy without theology, theology without science, science without either philosophy or theology, and each of these without the true humanism of the literary arts.[15]

Hope rooted in the incarnation of Christ made facing such a Herculean task possible and for public intellectuals to be useful to people they were called to serve.

FREE OF FEAR

Without hope, the tasks public intellectuals are called to bear would reasonably initiate fear. Hope for Hesburgh was made possible through the incarnation and the reenactment of Christ's sacrifice in the Mass. He thus believed he was marked by a sacramental character and ordained to a particular end—an end ultimately defined by the worship of God. Only then could he properly mediate between the eternal and the temporal, between God and humanity. As Hesburgh wrote in *The Theology of Catholic Action*, "This function of mediation looks both to God and to men: to God in worship and atonement for sin, the basis of disunity, and to men in order to bring them divine grace and truth in Christ, the center of unity."[16] The mediator looks in both directions, knowing the unity that defines one direction is what makes it possible for the disunity defining the other to be overcome.

In *A Companion to the Summa*, Dominican priest Walter Farrell noted that if fulfilling such a mediating role was "merely [a] human office, it would be a lonely, terrifying, comfortless thing to strike terror into the heart of man."[17] With hope, a hope made possible by the incarnation and the reenactment of Christ's sacrifice in the Mass, Hesburgh found such a calling to have "depths of serene joy that only God can sound."[18] Whether the challenge at hand is the proper use of nuclear energy or the proper receipt of displaced persons, the person God calls to mediate finds that "on the one side there will be the desperate, trusting dependence of these men, women, and children spurring him on; on the other, the unutterable perfection of God shining upon him with a brilliance that throws his every weakness into bold relief"; when called, however, human beings find the ability "to stand between God and the people."[19]

As previously noted, when called "to stand between God and people," human beings appreciate that the outcome does not solely depend upon their efforts, but upon God and the mysterious nature of God's understanding of how and when the temporal and the eternal will again become one. In the meantime, God calls all people to participate in the ongoing work of grace. Some people refuse the invitation to participate in that work while others agree to accept it. Christ mentioned this during his earthly ministry, as recorded in Matthew 9:35–38:

> Jesus went around to all the towns and villages, teaching in their synagogues, proclaiming the gospel of the kingdom, and curing every disease and illness. At the sight of the crowds, his heart was moved with pity for them because they were troubled and abandoned, like sheep without a shepherd. Then he said to his disciples, "The harvest is abundant but the laborers are few; so ask the master of the harvest to send out laborers for his harvest."

The laborers are few, in part, because many who are called do not embrace the purpose God offered them. The laborers who do respond learn that while their efforts are important, their efforts are secondary to their willingness to embrace the purpose God offered them and participate in the grace that makes all things possible.

Such an understanding of grace and one's participation in it did not lessen the expectations one had for achievement. If anything,

Hesburgh argued the opposite was true. Out of response to the grace Christ made possible via the incarnation and then reenacted in celebrating the Mass, dedication to whatever one was capable of offering was the only sufficient response. Hesburgh committed himself to such an understanding early in his presidency at Notre Dame. In an untitled address offered during those early years, Hesburgh argued the Catholic character of the university was, in fact, "being kept alive in an atmosphere that wants no mediocrity that would lessen the professional competence of the Notre Dame men of tomorrow, be they in business, engineering, science, or law."[20]

In a manner reminiscent of his 1962 *Time* cover story, Hesburgh went on to argue that "we want our men to know, love, and serve God. And how is God better glorified than by intelligent and devoted service to our fellow men, in the line of our chosen life's work."[21] In essence, mediocrity, especially mediocrity parading as Christian sentimentality, was not a worthy response to the sacrifice offered by one's Savior. Or, to echo the words of Christ as recorded in Luke 12:48, "Much will be required of the person entrusted with much, and still more will be demanded of the person entrusted with more."

Such an understanding of grace also compelled one to follow truth wherever truth demanded one follow. The incarnation had embedded within Christianity the understanding that history's end was decided. All that remained was how to live between now and then. As Hesburgh argued in that *Time* cover story, no conflict existed between science and theology. At any point in which conflict existed, bad science, bad theology, or perhaps both were present. Hesburgh believed mediation also demanded redemption and thus the Christian scholar, the Church's public intellectual, was often called to follow truth to places fear may otherwise dissuade one from going.

Quoting *Christianity and Philosophy* by Etienne Gilson, a prominent French philosopher and contemporary of Jacques Maritain, Hesburgh argued,

Without theology, we can indeed be, on the one hand Christians, and on the other hand savants, philosophers or artists, but never without theology will our Christianity descend into our science, into our philosophy, into our art, to reform them from within and vivify them. For that, the best will in the world would not suffice. It is necessary to know how to do it, in order to be able to do it, and like the rest it cannot be known without being learned.[22]

By fully participating in the grace Christ made possible, hope replaced fear in terms of where truth may lead. Pride might keep one from admitting, for example, to the practice of bad theology or science. However, Hesburgh believed the logical end of intellectual humility was that the unity of all truth was possible whether such an understanding occurred in one's lifetime or one rightly paved the way for others to follow. Fearing where truth may lead was thus nothing more than a subtle yet persistent denial of the life, death, and resurrection of Christ.

◊ ◊ ◊

As the Church's public intellectual, Hesburgh embraced the purpose God offered him. He also knew even his best efforts would prove incapable of meeting all the challenges God laid before him—challenges including science and technology, civil and human rights, economic development, ecumenical relations, immigration, and foreign relations. Regardless, by God's grace he embraced this tension. As a result, Hesburgh's favorite prayer, the one Father Jenkins briefly mentioned on February 27, 2015, when he notified the Notre Dame community of Hesburgh's passing, was printed on the back of the prayer cards issued at his funeral Mass.

Conclusion

Come Holy Spirit,
fill the hearts of your
faithful and kindle in them
the fire of your love.
Send forth your Spirit
and they shall be created.
And you shall renew
the face of the earth.

O, God, who by the
light of the Holy Spirit,
did instruct the hearts
of the faithful, grant that
by the same Holy Spirit
we may be truly wise and
ever enjoy his consolations,
Through Christ Our Lord,
Amen.

NOTES

PROLOGUE

1. Wilson D. Miscamble, *American Priest: The Ambitious Life and Conflicted Legacy of Notre Dame's Father Ted Hesburgh* (New York: Image Books, 2019), xviii.

2. Miscamble, *American Priest,* xviii.

3. Miscamble, *American Priest,* 97.

4. Miscamble, *American Priest,* 353.

5. Miscamble, *American Priest,* 377–78.

6. Miscamble, *American Priest,* 378.

7. John C. Lungren Jr., *Hesburgh of Notre Dame: Priest, Educator, Public Servant* (Kansas City, MO: Sheed and Ward, 1987), 137.

8. Lungren, *Hesburgh of Notre Dame,* 137.

INTRODUCTION

1. "Statement by Rev. John I. Jenkins, C.S.C., on the Death of Rev. Theodore M. Hesburgh, C.S.C.," University of Notre Dame Office of Public Relations and Communications, February 27, 2015, accessed April 27, 2020, https://news.nd.edu/news/statement-by-rev-john-i-jenkins-c-s-c-on-the -death-of-rev-theodore-m-hesburgh-c-s-c/.

2. Scott Jaschik, "Father Hesburgh Dies at 97," *Inside Higher Ed,* February 27, 2015, https://www.insidehighered.com/news/2015/02/27/ father-hesburgh-leader-notre-dame-and-american-higher-education-dies -97.

3. Anthony DePalma, "Rev. Theodore Hesburgh, 97, Dies; Lifted Notre Dame and Advised Presidents," *New York Times,* February 28, 2015, https://www.nytimes.com/2015/02/28/us/rev-theodore-hesburgh -influential-ex-president-of-notre-dame-dies-at-97.html.

4. Nick Anderson, "The Rev. Theodore Hesburgh, Ex-Notre Dame President, Dies at 97," *Washington Post,* February 27, 2105, https://www .washingtonpost.com/national/the-rev-theodore-hesburgh-ex-notre -dame-president-dies-at-97/2015/02/27/e1becf8a-be79-11e4-b274 -e5209a3bc9a9_story.html?noredirect=on&utm_term=.4aabdc328f3b.

5. Kate Thayer, "Theodore Hesburgh a Visionary President Who Transformed Notre Dame," *Chicago Tribune,* February 27, 2015, http:// www.chicagotribune.com/news/nationworld/chi-theodore-hesburgh-dead -20150227-story.html.

6. Tom Coyne, "Theodore Hesburgh Dies at 97; Priest Turned Notre Dame into Academic Power," *Los Angeles Times,* February 27, 2015, http:// www.latimes.com/local/obituaries/la-me-theodore-hesburgh-20150228 -story.html.

7. Sarah Mervosh, Megan Doyle, and Ann Marie Jakubowski, "Rev. Theodore M. Hesburgh, C.S.C.," *The Observer* 48, no. 98 (February 27, 2015): 1, http://www.archives.nd.edu/Observer/v48/2015-02-27_v48_098.pdf.

8. The White House of President Barack Obama, "Presidential Medal of Freedom," last updated 2016, accessed April 27, 2020, https:// obamawhitehouse.archives.gov/campaign/medal-of-freedom.

9. 106th Congress Pub. L. No. 106–153 (1999), https://www .govinfo.gov/content/pkg/PLAW-106publ153/html/PLAW-106publ153 .htm.

10. United States Postal Service, "U.S. Postal Service Honors Father Theodore Hesburgh, C.S.C. on a New Commemorative Forever Stamp on Sale Nationwide Today," September 1, 2017, accessed April 27, 2020, https://about.usps.com/news/national-releases/2017/pr17_047.htm.

11. "Father Hesburgh, Honorary Degrees," University of Notre Dame, accessed September 9, 2019, https://hesburgh.nd.edu/fr-teds-life/a-leader -in-higher-education/honorary-degrees/.

12. Aaron Blake, "Did Dianne Feinstein Accuse a Judicial Nominee of Being Too Christian?," *Washington Post,* September 7, 2017, https://www .washingtonpost.com/news/the-fix/wp/2017/09/07/did-a-democratic -senator-just-accuse-a-judicial-nominee-of-being-too-christian/?utm_term =.7e3c72e7d106.

Notes

13. Michelle Boorstein and Julie Zauzmer, "The Story behind Potential Supreme Court Nominee Amy Coney Barrett's Little-Known Catholic Group, People of Praise," *Washington Post,* July 7, 2018, https://www.washingtonpost.com/news/acts-of-faith/wp/2018/07/06/the-story-behind-potential-supreme-court-nominee-amy-coney-barretts-little-known-catholic-group-people-of-praise/.

14. Mary Clare Jalonick and Elana Schor, "No 'Dogma': Democrats Walk Tightrope on Barrett's Faith," *Associated Press,* October 10, 2020, https://apnews.com/article/donald-trump-ruth-bader-ginsburg-amy-coney-barrett-dianne-feinstein-judiciary-2aaf6821079ac0c5c6fe50699ad745ba.

15. Michael C. Desch, "Public Intellectuals: An Introduction," in *Public Intellectuals in the Global Arena: Professors or Pundits?,* ed. Michael C. Desch (Notre Dame, IN: University of Notre Dame Press, 2016), 1.

16. Richard A. Posner, *Public Intellectuals: A Study in Decline* (Chicago: University of Chicago Press, 2001), 3.

17. Posner, *Public Intellectuals,* 3.

18. Russell Jacoby, *The Last Intellectuals: American Culture in the Age of Academe* (New York: Basic Books, 2000), 3, 6.

19. John Michael, *Anxious Intellects: Academic Professionals, Public Intellectuals, and Enlightenment Values* (Durham, NC: Duke University Press, 2000), 1.

20. Michael, *Anxious Intellects,* 2.

21. Michael, *Anxious Intellects,* 2.

22. Amitai Etzioni, "Are Public Intellectuals an Endangered Species?" in *Public Intellectuals: An Endangered Species?,* ed. Amitai Etzioni and Alyssa Bowditch (Lanham, MD: Rowman & Littlefield, 2006), 21.

23. Jean Bethke Elshtain, "Why Public Intellectuals?" in *Public Intellectuals: An Endangered Species?,* ed. Amitai Etzioni and Alyssa Bowditch (Lanham, MD: Rowman & Littlefield, 2006), 82.

24. Elshtain, "Why Public Intellectuals?," 84.

25. Theodore M. Hesburgh, "Where Are College Presidents' Voices on Important Public Issues?," *Chronicle of Higher Education,* February 2, 2001, https://www.chronicle.com/article/Where-Are-College-Presidents/24966.

26. Hesburgh, "Where Are College Presidents?"

27. Hesburgh, "Where Are College Presidents?"

28. James M. O'Toole, *The Faithful: A History of Catholics in America* (Cambridge, MA: Belknap, 2008), 13.

29. O'Toole, *The Faithful,* 139.

30. O'Toole, *The Faithful,* 144.

31. Paul Blanshard, *American Freedom and Catholic Power* (Boston, MA: Beacon Press, 1949), 72; John Courtney Murray, Review of *American Freedom and Catholic Power*, by Paul Blanshard, *Catholic World* 169 (June 1949), https://www.library.georgetown.edu/woodstock/murray/1949h.

32. Blanshard, *American Freedom*, 72.

33. Blanshard, *American Freedom*, 72.

34. Murray, Review of *American Freedom and Catholic Power*, 233.

35. An important overview of the discrimination Catholics in the United States faced is found in Gustavus Myers, *History of Bigotry in the United States* (New York: Random House, 1943).

36. Robert E. Burns, *Being Catholic, Being American: The Notre Dame Story, 1842–1934* (Notre Dame, IN: University of Notre Dame Press, 1999), 303.

37. Burns, *Being Catholic*, 315. For further details, see Todd Tucker, *Notre Dame vs. the Klan: How the Fighting Irish Defeated the Ku Klux Klan* (Chicago: Loyola Press, 2004).

38. Two helpful sources that unpack the changing roles Catholics shared with the U.S. presidency during the latter half of the twentieth century and the early portion of the twenty-first century are by the St. Norbert College historian Lawrence J. McAndrews: *What They Wished For: American Catholics and American Presidents, 1960–2004* (Athens: University of Georgia Press, 2014); *Refuge in the Lord: Catholics, Presidents, and the Politics of Immigration, 1981–2013* (Washington, DC: Catholic University of America Press, 2015).

39. For further biographical details, consider John Lungren Jr., *Hesburgh of Notre Dame: Priest, Educator, Public Servant* (Kansas City, MO: Sheed & Ward, 1987); Michael O'Brien, *Hesburgh: A Biography* (Washington, DC: Catholic University of America Press, 1998); Wilson D. Miscamble, CSC, *American Priest: The Ambitious Life and Conflicted Legacy of Notre Dame's Father Ted Hesburgh* (New York: Image, 2019). Jill A. Boughton and Julie Water, *God's Icebreaker: The Life and Adventures of Father Ted Hesburgh* (Notre Dame, IN: Corby Books, 2011) is a great biography for children. Robert Schmuhl, *Fifty Years with Father Hesburgh: On and Off the Record* (Notre Dame, IN: University of Notre Dame Press, 2016); and Digger Phelps (with Tim Bourret), *Father Ted Hesburgh: He Coached Me* (Chicago: Triumph Books, 2017) are memoirs worth considering.

40. On January 17, 1992, Pope John Paul II elevated the status of the Church of the Sacred Heart to a minor basilica.

41. "The Notre Dame President," The University of Notre Dame, accessed April 27, 2020, https://hesburgh.nd.edu/fr-teds-life/the-notre-dame-president/.

42. Theodore M. Hesburgh, interviewed by Todd C. Ream, Notre Dame, IN, April 11, 2014.

43. Theodore M. Hesburgh, "The Work of Mediation," *Commonweal*, 75 (October 6, 1961): 34.

44. Edward P. Hahnenberg's 2017 article "Theodore M. Hesburgh, Theologian: Revisiting Land O'Lakes Fifty Years Later," *Theological Studies* 78, no. 4: 930–59, proved to be an immensely helpful exploration of Hesburgh's calling as a mediator.

45. Theodore M. Hesburgh, "Reflections on Priesthood"—CPHS142-20-02, 3. Theodore Martin Hesburgh Papers (PHS), University of Notre Dame Archives (UNDA), Notre Dame, IN 46556.

46. Hesburgh, "Reflections on Priesthood."

CHAPTER I

1. Jacques Barzun, *The American University: How It Runs, Where It Is Going* (Chicago: University of Chicago Press, 1993), 210.

2. Frank M. Turner, "Editor's Preface," to John Henry Newman, *The Idea of a University* (New Haven, CT: Yale University Press, 1996), ix.

3. Todd C. Ream, "Tales from Two Cities: The Evolving Identity of John Henry Newman's *The Idea of a University*," *Newman Studies Journal* 4, no. 1 (2007): 24–37.

4. Theodore M. Hesburgh, "Introduction: The Challenge and Promise of a Catholic University," *The Challenge and Promise of a Catholic University*, ed. Theodore M. Hesburgh (Notre Dame, IN: University of Notre Dame Press, 1994), 3.

5. Theodore M. Hesburgh, "Untitled Address"—UDIS-H1-35-03, 4–5. Theodore Martin Hesburgh Papers (PHS), University of Notre Dame Archives (UNDA), Notre Dame, IN 46556.

6. Leo. R. Ward, *Blueprint for a Catholic University* (St. Louis: Herder, 1949).

7. Theodore M. Hesburgh, "Preface," to Leo R. Ward, *My Fifty Years at Notre Dame* (1978), accessed April 28, 2020, http://archives.nd.edu/ward/ward.htm.

8. John Tracy Ellis, "American Catholics and the Intellectual Life," *Thought* 30 (Autumn 1955): 2–3, https://www3.nd.edu/~afreddos/papers/ellis-1955.pdf.

9. Theodore M. Hesburgh (with Jerry Reedy), *God, Country, Notre Dame* (New York: Doubleday, 1990), 70.

10. Theodore M. Hesburgh, "Looking Back at Newman," *America* 106 (March 3, 1962): 720.

11. John Henry Newman, *The Idea of a University* (Notre Dame, IN: University of Notre Dame Press, 1960), 177.

12. "God & Man at Notre Dame," *Time*, February 9, 1962, 48.

13. "God & Man at Notre Dame," 48.

14. "God & Man at Notre Dame," 54.

15. Theodore M. Hesburgh, "Untitled Address"—CPHS141-09-03, 5. Theodore Martin Hesburgh Papers (PHS), University of Notre Dame Archives (UNDA), Notre Dame, IN 46556.

16. Theodore M. Hesburgh, "Untitled Address"—UDIS-H1-35-08, 4. Theodore Martin Hesburgh Papers (PHS), University of Notre Dame Archives (UNDA), Notre Dame, IN 46556.

17. Hesburgh, "Untitled Address"—CPHS141-09-03, 5.

18. Hesburgh, "Untitled Address"—UDIS-H1-35-08, 4.

19. Theodore M. Hesburgh, "Around the World"—CPHS-144-57, 29. Theodore Martin Hesburgh Papers (PHS), University of Notre Dame Archives (UNDA), Notre Dame, IN 46556.

20. Hesburgh, "Looking Back at Newman," 721.

21. Hesburgh, "Looking Back at Newman," 721.

22. Theodore M. Hesburgh, "Untitled Address"—CPHS141-09-03, 8. Theodore Martin Hesburgh Papers (PHS), University of Notre Dame Archives (UNDA), Notre Dame, IN 46556.

23. Hesburgh, "Untitled Address"—CPHS141-09-03, 8.

24. For further details, see John Courtney Murray, "On the Structure of the Church-State Problem," in *The Catholic Church in World Affairs*, ed. Waldemar Gurian and M. A. Fitzsimons (Notre Dame, IN: University of Notre Dame Press, 1954), 11–32.

25. Hesburgh (with Reedy), *God, Country, Notre Dame*, 224.

26. For details concerning Ottaviani's larger effort to silence Murray, see Robert Nugent, *Silence Speaks: Teilhard de Chardin, Yves Congar, John Courtney Murray, and Thomas Merton* (Mahwah, NJ: Paulist Press, 2011).

27. Hesburgh (with Reedy), *God, Country, Notre Dame*, 224.

28. Hesburgh (with Reedy), *God, Country, Notre Dame*, 225.

29. Hesburgh (with Reedy), *God, Country, Notre Dame*, 227.

30. Hesburgh (with Reedy), *God, Country, Notre Dame*, 227.

31. Hesburgh (with Reedy), *God, Country, Notre Dame*, 230.

32. Theodore M. Hesburgh, "Address to the Eighth General Conference of the International Federation of Catholic Universities"—CPHS142-01-09, 11. Theodore Martin Hesburgh Papers (PHS), University of Notre Dame Archives (UNDA), Notre Dame, IN 46556.

33. Neil G. McCluskey, "Preamble," in "The Land O' Lakes Statement: The Idea of the Catholic University" (1967), 3, https://cushwa.nd.edu/assets/245340/landolakesstatement.pdf.

34. "The Land O' Lakes Statement: The Idea of the Catholic University" (1967). Italics in original.

35. For examples of criticisms of Hesburgh's views, consider David L. Schindler, *Heart of the World, Center of the Church: Communio Ecclesiology, Liberalism, and Liberation* (Grand Rapids: Eerdmans, 1996); Wilson D. Miscamble, *For Notre Dame: Battling for the Heart and Soul of a Catholic University* (South Bend, IN: St. Augustine's Press, 2013); Charles E. Rice, *What Happened to Notre Dame?* (South Bend, IN: St. Augustine's Press, 2009).

36. Theodore M. Hesburgh, "Action in the Face of Student Violence," *Catholic Mind* 67 (April 1969): 14.

37. Hesburgh, "Action in the Face," 15.

38. Cliff Wintrode, "Five Students Expelled in CIA-Dow Protests, University Suspends Five Others," *The Observer*, November 20, 1969, 1.

39. Hesburgh, "Action in the Face of Student Violence," 18.

40. Theodore M. Hesburgh, "Reflections on a Church-Related University"—CPHS142-14-02, 11. Theodore Martin Hesburgh Papers (PHS), University of Notre Dame Archives (UNDA), Notre Dame, IN 46556.

CHAPTER 2

1. Fritz Thompson, "Locals Witnessed History in a Flash," *Albuquerque Journal*, Special Reprint, "Trinity: Fifty Years Later," July 16, 1995, 8.

2. Theodore M. Hesburgh, "Science and Man"—CPHS141-18-03, 5. Theodore Martin Hesburgh Papers (PHS), University of Notre Dame Archives (UNDA), Notre Dame, IN 46556.

3. Hesburgh, "Science and Man"—CPHS141-18-03, 2.

4. "About the NSB [National Science Board]," National Science Foundation, accessed September 10, 2019, https://www.nsf.gov/nsb/about/index.jsp.

5. Hesburgh, "Science and Man"—CPHS141-18-03, 3.

6. Theodore M. Hesburgh, "Science and Modern Man"—CPHS141-07-05, 4. Theodore Martin Hesburgh Papers (PHS), University of Notre Dame Archives (UNDA), Notre Dame, IN 46556.

7. Hesburgh, "Science and Modern Man"—CPHS141-07-05, 7.

8. Hesburgh, "Science and Modern Man"—CPHS141-07-05, 9.

9. Theodore M. Hesburgh, "Untitled Address"—CPHS 1411-10-05, 3. Theodore Martin Hesburgh Papers (PHS), University of Notre Dame Archives (UNDA), Notre Dame, IN 46556.

10. Hesburgh, "Science and Modern Man"—CPHS141-07-05, 10.

11. Hesburgh, "Science and Modern Man"—CPHS141-07-05, 8.

12. Hesburgh, "Science and Modern Man"—CPHS141-07-05, 4.

13. Hesburgh, "Science and Man"—CPHS141-09-04, 2.

14. Hesburgh, "Science and Man"—CPHS141-09-04, 2.

15. Hesburgh, "Science and Man"—CPHS141-09-04, 3.

16. Theodore M. Hesburgh, "Science and Man"—CPHS141-18-2, 2. Theodore Martin Hesburgh Papers (PHS), University of Notre Dame Archives (UNDA), Notre Dame, IN 46556.

17. Hesburgh, "Science and Man"—CPHS141-18-02, 2.

18. Hesburgh, "Science and Man"—CPHS141-18-02, 3.

19. Hesburgh, "Science and Man"—CPHS141-18-02, 9.

20. Hesburgh, "Science and Man"—CPHS141-18-03, 8.

21. Hesburgh, "Science and Man"—CPHS141-18-03, 12.

22. Hesburgh, "Science and Man"—CPHS141-18-03, 13.

23. Hesburgh, "Science and Man"—CPHS141-18-03, 12.

24. Hesburgh, "Science and Man"—CPHS141-09-04, 4.

25. One of Hesburgh's most thorough treatments of the threat posed by the Cold War and the nuclear threat is found in his offering for Carnegie Council on Ethics and International Affairs' Morgenthau Memorial Lecture in New York City on November 3, 1988. Theodore M. Hesburgh, "Untitled Address"—CPHS142-25-02. Theodore Martin Hesburgh Papers (PHS), University of Notre Dame Archives (UNDA), Notre Dame, IN 46556.

26. Hesburgh, "Science and Man"—CPHS141-09-04, 7.

27. Theodore Martin Hesburgh. "The Future of Liberal Education"—CPHS142-15-01, 7. Theodore Martin Hesburgh Papers (PHS), University of Notre Dame Archives (UNDA), Notre Dame, IN 46556.

28. Hesburgh, "The Future of Liberal Education"—CPHS142-15-01, 9.

29. Hesburgh, "The Future of Liberal Education"—CPHS142-15-01, 12.

30. Hesburgh, "Science and Man"—CPHS141-18-03, 7.

31. Theodore M. Hesburgh, "Science and Technology in Modern Perspective"—CPHS141-18-03, 12. Theodore Martin Hesburgh Papers (PHS), University of Notre Dame Archives (UNDA), Notre Dame, IN 46556.

32. Theodore M. Hesburgh, "Untitled Address"—CPHS143-02-09, 1. Theodore Martin Hesburgh Papers (PHS), University of Notre Dame Archives (UNDA), Notre Dame, IN 46556.

33. Hesburgh, "Untitled Address"—CPHS143-02-09, 3.

34. Hesburgh, "Science and Man"—CPHS141-18-03, 9.

35. Hesburgh, "Science and Man"—CPHS141-18-03, 10.

36. Theodore M. Hesburgh, "Science and Technology in Modern Perspective"—CPHS141-18-02, 5. Theodore Martin Hesburgh Papers (PHS), University of Notre Dame Archives (UNDA), Notre Dame, IN 46556.

37. Hesburgh, "Science and Technology in Modern Perspective"—CPHS141-18-02, 6.

38. Hesburgh, "Science and Man"—CPHS141-18-03, 12.

39. Hesburgh, "Science and Technology in Modern Perspective"—CPHS141-18-02, 6.

40. Hesburgh, "Science and Technology in Modern Perspective"—CPHS141-18-02, 6–7.

CHAPTER 3

1. James H. Madison, *A Lynching in the Heartland: Race and Memory in America* (New York: Palgrave, 2001), 8–11.

2. James H. Madison, *Hoosiers: A New History of Indiana* (Bloomington: Indiana University Press, 2014), 314.

3. Theodore M. Hesburgh (with Jerry Reedy), *God, Country, Notre Dame* (New York: Doubleday, 1990), 190.

4. Theodore M. Hesburgh, "Statement of Theodore M. Hesburgh, C.S.C., Chairman, United States Commission on Civil Rights before the Subcommittee on Administrative Practices and Procedures, Committee on the Judiciary, United States Senate, June 23, 1971"—CPHS143-09-02, 2. Theodore Martin Hesburgh Papers (PHS), University of Notre Dame Archives (UNDA), Notre Dame, IN 46556.

5. For a more detailed discussion of the efforts of the Civil Rights Commission, see Foster Rhea Dulles, *The Civil Rights Commission: 1957–*

1965 (East Lansing: Michigan State University Press, 1968). For more detailed discussions of the civil rights movement, see Bruce Ackerman, *We the People, Vol. 3: The Civil Rights Revolution* (Cambridge, MA: Belknap, 2014); Taylor Branch (3 vols.), *Parting the Waters: America in the King Years, 1954–1963* (New York: Simon & Schuster, 1988); *Pillar of Fire: America in the King Years, 1963–1965* (New York: Simon & Schuster, 1998); and *At Canaan's Edge: America in the King Years, 1965–1968* (New York: Simon & Schuster, 2006).

6. Hesburgh, "Statement of Theodore M. Hesburgh, C.S.C., Chairman, United States Commission on Civil Rights before the Subcommittee on Administrative Practices and Procedures, Committee on the Judiciary, United States Senate, June 23, 1971"—CPHS143-09-02, 1.

7. Theodore M. Hesburgh, "Untitled Address"—CPHS142-21-05, 4. Theodore Martin Hesburgh Papers (PHS), University of Notre Dame Archives (UNDA), Notre Dame, IN 46556.

8. United States Civil Rights Commission, *Hearings before the United States Commission on Civil Rights—Hearings Held in Jackson, MS, February 16–20, 1965* (Washington, DC: Government Printing Office, n.d.), 59–61.

9. Theodore M. Hesburgh, "Untitled Address"—CPHS142-21-05, 4. Theodore Martin Hesburgh Papers (PHS), University of Notre Dame Archives (UNDA), Notre Dame, IN 46556.

10. Hesburgh, "Untitled Address"—CPHS142-21-05, 4.

11. Theodore M. Hesburgh, "Social Responsibility of Graduate Education"—CPHS142-21-04, 10. Theodore Martin Hesburgh Papers (PHS), University of Notre Dame Archives (UNDA), Notre Dame, IN 46556.

12. Hesburgh, "Untitled Address"—CPHS142-21-05, 6.

13. Charles Y. and Ellen Siegelman, eds., *Prejudice, U.S.A.* (New York: Praeger, 1969). Theodore M. Hesburgh, "Foreword"—CPHS142-01-01, 1. Theodore Martin Hesburgh Papers (PHS), University of Notre Dame Archives (UNDA), Notre Dame, IN 46556.

14. Hesburgh, "Foreword"—CPHS142-01-01, 2.

15. Hesburgh, "Foreword"—CPHS142-01-01, 3.

16. Hesburgh, "Foreword"—CPHS142-01-01, 3–4.

17. Hesburgh, "Foreword"—CPHS142-01-01, 5.

18. Hesburgh, "Foreword"—CPHS142-01-01, 9.

19. Hesburgh, "Foreword"—CPHS142-01-01, 8.

20. Hesburgh, "Foreword"—CPHS142-01-01, 7.

21. Theodore M. Hesburgh, "Untitled Address"—CPHS141-15-03, 10. Theodore Martin Hesburgh Papers (PHS), University of Notre Dame Archives (UNDA), Notre Dame, IN 46556.

22. Hesburgh, "Untitled Address"—CPHS141-15-03, 11.

23. Hesburgh, "Untitled Address"—CPHS141-15-03, 10.

24. Hesburgh, "Untitled Address"—CPHS141-15-03, 13.

25. Hesburgh, "Untitled Address"—CPHS141-15-03, 14.

26. Hesburgh, "Untitled Address"—CPHS141-15-03, 14.

27. Theodore M. Hesburgh, "Untitled Address"—CPHS141-21-03, 4. Theodore Martin Hesburgh Papers (PHS), University of Notre Dame Archives (UNDA), Notre Dame, IN 46556.

28. Hesburgh, "Untitled Address"—CPHS141-21-03, 5.

29. Hesburgh, "Untitled Address"—CPHS141-21-03, 5–6.

30. Theodore M. Hesburgh, "The Moral Dimensions of the Civil Rights Movement"—CPHS141-21-08, 8–9. Theodore Martin Hesburgh Papers (PHS), University of Notre Dame Archives (UNDA), Notre Dame, IN 46556.

31. Hesburgh, "The Moral Dimensions of the Civil Rights Movement"—CPHS141-21-08, 9.

32. Hesburgh, "The Moral Dimensions of the Civil Rights Movement"—CPHS141-21-08, 10.

33. Hesburgh, "The Moral Dimensions of the Civil Rights Movement"—CPHS141-21-08, 16.

34. Hesburgh, "The Moral Dimensions of the Civil Rights Movement"—CPHS141-21-08, 19.

35. Hesburgh, "The Moral Dimensions of the Civil Rights Movement"—CPHS141-21-08, 21–22.

36. Hesburgh, "The Moral Dimensions of the Civil Rights Movement"—CPHS141-21-08, 23–24.

37. Hesburgh, "The Moral Dimensions of the Civil Rights Movement"—CPHS141-21-08, 24–26.

38. Hesburgh, "The Moral Dimensions of the Civil Rights Movement"—CPHS141-21-08, 27.

39. Theodore M. Hesburgh, "Untitled Address"—CPHS141-23-02, 4. Theodore Martin Hesburgh Papers (PHS), University of Notre Dame Archives (UNDA), Notre Dame, IN 46556.

40. Theodore M. Hesburgh, "Statement of the Reverend Theodore M. Hesburgh, C.S.C. President, University of Notre Dame before the Subcommittee on International Organizations and Movements, Foreign

Affairs Committee, United States House of Representatives, October 11, 1973"—CPHS143-09-01, 5-6. Theodore Martin Hesburgh Papers (PHS), University of Notre Dame Archives (UNDA), Notre Dame, IN 46556.

41. Jimmy Carter, "Notre Dame Commencement Speech." Folder Citation: Collection: Office of Staff Secretary; Series: Presidential Files; Folder: 5/22/77; Container: 21; 4.

42. Carter, "Notre Dame Commencement Speech," 1–2.

43. Carter, "Notre Dame Commencement Speech," 5.

44. Carter, "Notre Dame Commencement Speech," 6.

45. Theodore M. Hesburgh, "Untitled Address"—CPHS142-04-08, 4. Theodore Martin Hesburgh Papers (PHS), University of Notre Dame Archives (UNDA), Notre Dame, IN 46556.

46. Hesburgh, "Untitled Address"—CPHS142-04-08, 4.

47. Theodore M. Hesburgh, "Untitled Address"—CPHS142-06-06, 6. Theodore Martin Hesburgh Papers (PHS), University of Notre Dame Archives (UNDA), Notre Dame, IN 46556.

48. Theodore M. Hesburgh, "Guess Who's for the ERA?"—CPHS142-09-01, n.p. Theodore Martin Hesburgh Papers (PHS), University of Notre Dame Archives (UNDA), Notre Dame, IN 46556.

49. Theodore M. Hesburgh, "Civil Rights and the Women's Movement"—CPHS143-01-06, 10–12. Theodore Martin Hesburgh Papers (PHS), University of Notre Dame Archives (UNDA), Notre Dame, IN 46556.

50. For example, see Wilson D. Miscamble, *American Priest: The Ambitious Life and Conflicted Legacy of Notre Dame's Father Ted Hesburgh* (New York: Image, 2019), 184–85, 301–2, 334–35.

51. Theodore M. Hesburgh, *The Humane Imperative: A Challenge for the Year 2000* (New Haven, CT: Yale University Press, 1974), 33.

52. Miscamble, *American Priest*, 154.

53. Hesburgh, "Guess Who's for the ERA?"—CPHS142-09-01, n.p.

54. Theodore M. Hesburgh, "Pro Life from a Social Justice Perspective"—CPHS143-03-04, 4. Theodore Martin Hesburgh Papers (PHS), University of Notre Dame Archives (UNDA), Notre Dame, IN 46556.

55. Theodore M. Hesburgh, "Pro Life from a Social Justice Perspective"—CPHS143-03-04, 7.

56. Madison, *Hoosiers*, 314.

CHAPTER 4

1. John W. O'Malley, *What Happened at Vatican II* (Cambridge, MA: Belknap, 2008), 15.

2. O'Malley, *What Happened at Vatican II*, 18.

3. O'Malley, *What Happened at Vatican II*, 21.

4. Peter Hebblethwaite, *Paul VI: The First Modern Pope* (Mahwah, NJ: Paulist Press, 2018), xiii.

5. O'Malley, *What Happened at Vatican II*, 2.

6. Edward Idris Cardinal Cassidy, *Ecumenism and Interreligious Dialogue* (Mahwah, NJ: Paulist Press, 2005), 10.

7. Theodore M. Hesburgh, "Untitled Address"—CPHS142-01-11, 3. Theodore Martin Hesburgh Papers (PHS), University of Notre Dame Archives (UNDA), Notre Dame, IN 46556.

8. Theodore M. Hesburgh, *The Humane Imperative: A Challenge for the Year 2000* (New Haven, CT: Yale University Press, 1974), 17.

9. Theodore M. Hesburgh, "Untitled Address"—CPHS142-26-01, 1–2. Theodore Martin Hesburgh Papers (PHS), University of Notre Dame Archives (UNDA), Notre Dame, IN 46556.

10. Hesburgh, "Untitled Address"—CPHS142-26-01, 2.

11. Hesburgh, "Untitled Address"—CPHS142-26-01, 2.

12. Hesburgh, "Untitled Address"—CPHS142-26-01, 2–3.

13. Hesburgh, "Untitled Address"—CPHS142-26-01, 3.

14. Hesburgh, "Untitled Address"—CPHS142-26-01, 4.

15. Hesburgh, "Untitled Address"—CPHS142-26-01, 4.

16. "Knights and Dames with a Mission to Care," Sovereign Order of Malta, accessed September 12, 2019, https://www.orderofmalta.int/sovereign-order-of-malta/knights-of-malta/.

17. Hesburgh, "Untitled Address"—CPHS142-26-01, 4.

18. Hesburgh, "Untitled Address"—CPHS142-26-01, 5.

19. Theodore M. Hesburgh, "Untitled Address"—CPHS142-06-08, 6. Theodore Martin Hesburgh Papers (PHS), University of Notre Dame Archives (UNDA), Notre Dame, IN 46556.

20. Hesburgh, "Untitled Address"—CPHS142-26-01, 5.

21. Hesburgh, "Untitled Address"—CPHS142-26-01, 5.

22. Theodore M. Hesburgh, "Preface," in *Hope of Unity: Living Ecumenism Today—Celebrating 40 Years of the Ecumenical Institute Tantur*, ed. Timothy S. Lowe (Berlin, Germany: AphorismA, 2013), 6.

23. Theodore M. Hesburgh, *God and the World of Man* (Notre Dame, IN: University of Notre Dame Press, 1950), 220.

24. Hesburgh, *God and the World of Man*, 221.

25. Hesburgh, *God and the World of Man*, 232.

26. Theodore M. Hesburgh, "The Historical Evolution of the Catholic View of Luther"—CPHS141-26-03, 3. Theodore Martin Hesburgh Papers (PHS), University of Notre Dame Archives (UNDA), Notre Dame, IN 46556.

27. Hesburgh, "The Historical Evolution of the Catholic View of Luther"—CPHS141-26-03, 3.

28. Hesburgh, "The Historical Evolution of the Catholic View of Luther"—CPHS141-26-03, 19-20.

29. Theodore M. Hesburgh, "Catholic Higher Education in Twentieth Century America"—CPHS141-16-04, 8. Theodore Martin Hesburgh Papers (PHS), University of Notre Dame Archives (UNDA), Notre Dame, IN 46556.

30. Hesburgh, "Catholic Higher Education in Twentieth Century America"—CPHS141-16-04, 8.

31. Hesburgh, "Catholic Higher Education in Twentieth Century America"—CPHS141-16-04, 9-10.

32. Hesburgh, "Catholic Higher Education in Twentieth Century America"—CPHS141-16-04, 10.

33. Hesburgh, "Catholic Higher Education in Twentieth Century America"—CPHS141-16-04, 11.

34. Theodore M. Hesburgh. "Untitled Address"—CPHS141-24-01, 4. Theodore Martin Hesburgh Papers (PHS), University of Notre Dame Archives (UNDA), Notre Dame, IN 46556.

35. Hesburgh, "Untitled Address"—CPHS141-24-01, 4.

36. Hesburgh, "Untitled Address"—CPHS141-24-01, 4.

37. Hesburgh, "Untitled Address"—CPHS141-24-01, 3.

38. Hesburgh, "Untitled Address"—CPHS141-24-01, 3.

39. Hesburgh, "Untitled Address"—CPHS141-24-01, 5.

40. Hesburgh would later share comparable forms of this argument against Cox's thesis in the commencement address at the Church of the Brethren's Manchester College. See Theodore M. Hesburgh, "Service: The Great Modern Prayer"—CPHS141-26-02. Theodore Martin Hesburgh Papers (PHS), University of Notre Dame Archives (UNDA), Notre Dame, IN 46556. Also at the Church of God's Anderson College. See Theodore M. Hesburgh, "Untitled Address"—CPHS142-03-04. Theodore Martin Hes-

burgh Papers (PHS), University of Notre Dame Archives (UNDA), Notre Dame, IN 46556.

41. Hesburgh, "Untitled Address"—CPHS141-26-01, 6.

42. Hesburgh, "Untitled Address"—CPHS141-26-01, 9.

43. Hesburgh, "Untitled Address"—CPHS141-26-01, 15–16.

44. Theodore M. Hesburgh, "The Changing Face of Catholic Higher Education"—CPHS142-02-02, 1. Theodore Martin Hesburgh Papers (PHS), University of Notre Dame Archives (UNDA), Notre Dame, IN 46556.

45. Hesburgh, "The Changing Face of Catholic Higher Education"—CPHS142-02-02, 2.

46. Hesburgh, "The Changing Face of Catholic Higher Education"—CPHS142-02-02, 2.

47. Hesburgh, "The Changing Face of Catholic Higher Education"—CPHS142-02-02, 6.

48. Hesburgh, "The Changing Face of Catholic Higher Education"—CPHS142-02-02, 7.

49. Hesburgh, "The Changing Face of Catholic Higher Education"—CPHS142-02-02, 9.

50. Hesburgh, "The Changing Face of Catholic Higher Education"—CPHS142-02-02, 11.

51. Hesburgh, "The Changing Face of Catholic Higher Education"—CPHS142-02-02, 13.

52. Hesburgh, "The Changing Face of Catholic Higher Education"—CPHS142-02-02, 16.

53. Hesburgh, "The Changing Face of Catholic Higher Education"—CPHS142-02-02, 18.

54. Theodore M. Hesburgh, "Untitled Address"—CPHS142-22-04, 5. Theodore Martin Hesburgh Papers (PHS), University of Notre Dame Archives (UNDA), Notre Dame, IN 46556.

55. Hesburgh, "Untitled Address"—CPHS142-22-04, 9.

56. Theodore M. Hesburgh, "Untitled Address"—CPHS142-25-01, 2. Theodore Martin Hesburgh Papers (PHS), University of Notre Dame Archives (UNDA), Notre Dame, IN 46556.

57. Hesburgh, "Untitled Address"—CPHS142-25-01, 4.

58. Hesburgh, "Untitled Address"—CPHS142-25-01, 3.

59. Theodore M. Hesburgh, "Untitled Address"—CPHS142-01-09, 1. Theodore Martin Hesburgh Papers (PHS), University of Notre Dame Archives (UNDA), Notre Dame, IN 46556.

60. Hesburgh, "Untitled Address"—CPHS142-01-09, 13-14.

61. Theodore M. Hesburgh, "Untitled Address"—CPHS142-07-03, 6. Theodore Martin Hesburgh Papers (PHS), University of Notre Dame Archives (UNDA), Notre Dame, IN 46556.

62. Hesburgh, "Untitled Address"—CPHS142-07-03, 23.

63. Hesburgh, "Untitled Address"—CPHS142-07-03, 25.

64. Theodore M. Hesburgh, "The Catholic University in the Modern Context"—CPHS142-12-06, 11. Theodore Martin Hesburgh Papers (PHS), University of Notre Dame Archives (UNDA), Notre Dame, IN 46556.

65. Hesburgh, "The Catholic University in the Modern Context"—CPHS142-12-06, 11–12.

66. Paul VI, *Ecclesiam Suam* (His Own Church), Encyclical Letter, August 6, 1964, http://w2.vatican.va/content/paul-vi/en/encyclicals/documents/hf_p-vi_enc_06081964_ecclesiam.htm.

67. See Matthew Levering, *An Introduction to Vatican II: As an Ongoing Theological Event* (Washington, DC: Catholic University of America Press, 2017).

CHAPTER 5

1. Theodore M. Hesburgh, "Untitled Address"—CPHS142-04-02, 19. Theodore Martin Hesburgh Papers (PHS), University of Notre Dame Archives (UNDA), Notre Dame, IN 46556.

2. Theodore M. Hesburgh, "Untitled Address"—CPHS142-21-05, 6. Theodore Martin Hesburgh Papers (PHS), University of Notre Dame Archives (UNDA), Notre Dame, IN 46556.

3. See Wilson D. Miscamble, *American Priest: The Ambitious Life and Conflicted Legacy of Notre Dame's Father Ted Hesburgh* (New York: Image, 2019), 103, 185.

4. Theodore M. Hesburgh (with Jerry Reedy), *God, Country, Notre Dame* (New York: Doubleday, 1990), 93–94.

5. Hesburgh (with Reedy), *God, Country, Notre Dame*, 96.

6. Theodore M. Hesburgh, "The Cultural and Educational Aspects of Development"—CPHS141-21-05, 5. Theodore Martin Hesburgh Papers (PHS), University of Notre Dame Archives (UNDA), Notre Dame, IN 46556.

7. Hesburgh, "The Cultural and Educational Aspects of Development"—CPHS141-21-05, 5.

8. Hesburgh, "The Cultural and Educational Aspects of Development"—CPHS141-21-05, 7.

9. Hesburgh, "The Cultural and Educational Aspects of Development"—CPHS141-21-05, 7.

10. Hesburgh, "The Cultural and Educational Aspects of Development"—CPHS141-21-05, 8.

11. Hesburgh, "The Cultural and Educational Aspects of Development"—CPHS141-21-05, 9.

12. Hesburgh, "The Cultural and Educational Aspects of Development"—CPHS141-21-05, 31–32.

13. Theodore M. Hesburgh, "The University in a World of Change"—CPHS141-21-09, 13. Theodore Martin Hesburgh Papers (PHS), University of Notre Dame Archives (UNDA), Notre Dame, IN 46556.

14. Theodore M. Hesburgh, "Untitled Address"—CPHS141-23-02, 4–5. Theodore Martin Hesburgh Papers (PHS), University of Notre Dame Archives (UNDA), Notre Dame, IN 46556.

15. For a more detailed discussion of Hesburgh's understanding of commitment, compassion, and consecration, see Theodore M. Hesburgh, "Colgate University Baccalaureate Address"—CPHS142-20-01. The full text of that address focuses on those three themes.

16. Theodore M. Hesburgh, "Our Stake in America"—CPHS141-21-02, 2. Theodore Martin Hesburgh Papers (PHS), University of Notre Dame Archives (UNDA), Notre Dame, IN 46556.

17. Hesburgh, "Our Stake in America"—CPHS141-21-02, 9.

18. Hesburgh, "Our Stake in America"—CPHS141-21-02, 13–14.

19. Theodore M. Hesburgh, "The Social Sciences in an Age of Social Revolution"—CPHS141-24-02, 6. Theodore Martin Hesburgh Papers (PHS), University of Notre Dame Archives (UNDA), Notre Dame, IN 46556.

20. Hesburgh, "The Social Sciences in an Age of Social Revolution"—CPHS141-24-02, 11.

21. Hesburgh, "The Social Sciences in an Age of Social Revolution"—CPHS141-24-02, 11.

22. Maritain, cited in Hesburgh, "The Social Sciences in an Age of Social Revolution"—CPHS141-24-02, 13.

23. Hesburgh, "The Social Sciences in an Age of Social Revolution"—CPHS141-24-02, 14.

24. Barbara Ward, *Spaceship Earth* (New York: Columbia University Press, 1966), vii.

25. Hesburgh, "The Social Sciences in an Age of Social Revolution"—CPHS141-24-02, 19–20.

26. Theodore M. Hesburgh, "In Defense of the Younger Generation"—CPHS142-01-08, 7. Theodore Martin Hesburgh Papers (PHS), University of Notre Dame Archives (UNDA), Notre Dame, IN 46556.

27. Theodore M. Hesburgh. "In Defense of the Younger Generation"—CPHS142-01-08, 6.

28. Theodore M. Hesburgh. "In Defense of the Younger Generation"—CPHS142-01-08, 9–10.

29. Theodore M. Hesburgh, "Untitled Address"—CPHS142-02-04, 2. Theodore Martin Hesburgh Papers (PHS), University of Notre Dame Archives (UNDA), Notre Dame, IN 46556.

30. Hesburgh, "Untitled Address"—CPHS142-02-04, 3–4.

31. Hesburgh, "Untitled Address"—CPHS142-02-04, 2–3.

32. Theodore M. Hesburgh, "Untitled Address"—CPHS142-04-02, 10. Theodore Martin Hesburgh Papers (PHS), University of Notre Dame Archives (UNDA), Notre Dame, IN 46556.

33. Hesburgh, "Untitled Address"—CPHS142-04-02, 1.

34. Hesburgh, "Untitled Address"—CPHS142-04-02, 3.

35. Hesburgh, "Untitled Address"—CPHS142-04-02, 7.

36. Hesburgh, "Untitled Address"—CPHS142-04-02, 16a.

37. Theodore M. Hesburgh, "A New Vision for Spaceship Earth"—CPHS143-10-01, 5. Theodore Martin Hesburgh Papers (PHS), University of Notre Dame Archives (UNDA), Notre Dame, IN 46556.

38. Hesburgh, "A New Vision for Spaceship Earth"—CPHS143-10-01, 12.

39. Hesburgh, "A New Vision for Spaceship Earth"—CPHS143-10-01, 13.

40. Hesburgh, "Food in an Interdependent World"—CPHS142-08-01, 1. Theodore Martin Hesburgh Papers (PHS), University of Notre Dame Archives (UNDA), Notre Dame, IN 46556.

41. Hesburgh, "Food in an Interdependent World"—CPHS142-08-01, 3.

42. Hesburgh, "Food in an Interdependent World"—CPHS142-08-01, 4.

43. Hesburgh, "Food in an Interdependent World"—CPHS142-08-01, 7.

44. Theodore M. Hesburgh, "A New Vision for the Year 2000"—CPHS142-12-03, 8. Theodore Martin Hesburgh Papers (PHS), University of Notre Dame Archives (UNDA), Notre Dame, IN 46556.

45. Ward cited in Theodore M. Hesburgh, *The Humane Imperative: A Challenge for the Year 2000* (New Haven, CT: Yale University Press, 1974), 100.

46. Hesburgh, *Humane Imperative*, 109.

47. Theodore M. Hesburgh, "Multinational Managers and Poverty in the Third World"—CPHS142-12-12, 11. Theodore Martin Hesburgh Papers (PHS), University of Notre Dame Archives (UNDA), Notre Dame, IN 46556.

48. Hesburgh, "Multinational Managers and Poverty in the Third World"—CPHS142-12-12, 13.

49. Hesburgh, "Multinational Managers and Poverty in the Third World"—CPHS142-12-12, ADD.

50. Theodore M. Hesburgh, "The Future of Liberal Education"—CPHS142-15-01, 4. Theodore Martin Hesburgh Papers (PHS), University of Notre Dame Archives (UNDA), Notre Dame, IN 46556.

51. "About Us," Andean Health and Development, accessed September 13, 2019, https://www.andeanhealth.org/about-us/. For a complete overview of Andean Health and Development, see Tony Hiss, *Long Road from Quito: Transforming Health Care in Rural Latin America* (Notre Dame, IN: University of Notre Dame Press, 2019).

52. Ann Kovar Miller, "ND Alum Opens Hesburgh Hospital in Ecuador," University of Notre Dame, accessed September 13, 2019, http://my.nd.edu/s/1210/myND/interior-2col.aspx?sid=1210&gid=1&pgid=21373&cid=41728&ecid=41728&crid=0&calpgid=18670&calcid=38645.

53. David Gaus, "ND Alum Opens Hesburgh Hospital in Ecuador," University of Notre Dame.

CHAPTER 6

1. James Phillips, "ICE Raids Poultry Plants," *Scott County Times*, August 14, 2019, https://www.sctonline.net/front-page-slideshow-news/ice-raids-poultry-plants#sthash.xb5ZQctj.Ae5v1R25.dpbs.

2. *PBS NewsHour*, "Why Massive Mississippi ICE Raids Took Communities by Surprise," August 8, 2019, https://www.pbs.org/newshour/show/why-massive-mississippi-ice-raids-took-communities-by-surprise.

3. Phillips, "ICE Raids Poultry Plants."

4. Phillips, "ICE Raids Poultry Plants."

5. *PBS NewsHour*, "Why Massive Mississippi ICE Raids."

6. Theodore M. Hesburgh, "Untitled Address"—CPHS142-18-03, 3. Theodore Martin Hesburgh Papers (PHS), University of Notre Dame Archives (UNDA), Notre Dame, IN 46556.

7. See Don Oberdorfer, "69 Million Cambodian Aid Pledged," *Washington Post*, October 25, 1979, https://www.washingtonpost.com/archive/politics/1979/10/25/69-million-cambodian-aid-pledged/26781a33-0ff2-4584-b1d3-03f30ca489ea/?noredirect=on; Theodore M. Hesburgh, "Voluntarism: An American Legacy"—CPHS142-15-0. Theodore Martin Hesburgh Papers (PHS), University of Notre Dame Archives (UNDA), Notre Dame, IN 46556.

8. Hesburgh, "Untitled Address"—CPHS142-18-03, 8.

9. Hesburgh, "Untitled Address"—CPHS142-18-03, 9–10.

10. Theodore M. Hesburgh, "Untitled Address"—CPHS142-23-01, 4. Theodore Martin Hesburgh Papers (PHS), University of Notre Dame Archives (UNDA), Notre Dame, IN 46556.

11. Hesburgh, "Untitled Address"—CPHS142-23-01, 2.

12. Hesburgh, "Untitled Address"—CPHS142-18-03, 1.

13. Hesburgh, "Untitled Address"—CPHS142-18-03, 2.

14. Hesburgh, "Untitled Address"—CPHS142-18-03, 2.

15. Hesburgh, "Untitled Address"—CPHS142-18-03, 2.

16. Hesburgh, "Untitled Address"—CPHS142-18-03, 4.

17. Hesburgh, "Untitled Address"—CPHS142-18-03, 2.

18. Theodore M. Hesburgh (with Jerry Reedy), *God, Country, Notre Dame* (Notre Dame, IN: University of Notre Dame Press, 1999), 276.

19. Hesburgh, "Untitled Address"—CPHS142-18-03, 5–6.

20. Hesburgh, "Untitled Address"—CPHS142-18-03, 6.

21. Hesburgh, "Untitled Address"—CPHS142-18-03, 6.

22. Hesburgh, "Untitled Address"—CPHS142-18-03, 6–7.

23. Hesburgh, "Untitled Address"—CPHS142-18-03, 7.

24. Hesburgh, "Untitled Address"—CPHS142-18-03, 7.

25. Hesburgh (with Reedy), *God, Country, Notre Dame*, 276.

26. Hesburgh (with Reedy), *God, Country, Notre Dame*, 277.

27. Jimmy Carter, "State of the Union Address 1981," January 16, 1981, § Refugees, https://www.jimmycarterlibrary.gov/assets/documents/speeches/su81jec.phtml.

28. Carter, "State of the Union Address 1981."

29. Hesburgh (with Reedy), *God, Country, Notre Dame*, 278.

30. Hesburgh, "Untitled Address"—CPHS142-18-03, 9.

31. Theodore M. Hesburgh, "Science and Technology in Modern Perspective"—CPHS141-18-02, 5–6. Theodore Martin Hesburgh Papers (PHS), University of Notre Dame Archives (UNDA), Notre Dame, IN 46556.

32. Theodore M. Hesburgh, "The Problems and Opportunities of a Very Interdependent Planet"—CPHS142-07-04, 6. Theodore Martin Hesburgh Papers (PHS), University of Notre Dame Archives (UNDA), Notre Dame, IN 46556.

33. Hesburgh. "The Problems and Opportunities of a Very Interdependent Planet"—CPHS142-07-04, 6.

34. Hesburgh, "The Problems and Opportunities of a Very Interdependent Planet"—CPHS142-07-04, 13.

35. Hesburgh, "The Problems and Opportunities of a Very Interdependent Planet"—CPHS142-07-04, 14.

36. Hesburgh, "The Problems and Opportunities of a Very Interdependent Planet"—CPHS142-07-04, 16.

37. Hesburgh, "The Problems and Opportunities of a Very Interdependent Planet"—CPHS142-07-04, 18.

38. Theodore M. Hesburgh, "Untitled Address"—CPHS142-18-07, 2. Theodore Martin Hesburgh Papers (PHS), University of Notre Dame Archives (UNDA), Notre Dame, IN 46556.

39. Hesburgh, "Untitled Address"—CPHS142-18-07, 2.

40. Hesburgh, "Untitled Address"—CPHS142-18-07, 3.

41. Hesburgh, "Untitled Address"—CPHS142-18-07, 12.

42. Leo XIII, *Rerum Novarum* (Rights and Duties of Capital and Labor), Encyclical Letter, May 15, 1891, http://www.vatican.va/content/leo-xiii/en/encyclicals/documents/hf_l-xiii_enc_15051891_rerum-novarum.html.

43. John Paul II, *Laborem Exercens* (Through Work), Encyclical Letter, September 14, 1981, http://www.vatican.va/content/john-paul-ii/en/encyclicals/documents/hf_jp-ii_enc_14091981_laborem-exercens.html.

44. Theodore M. Hesburgh, "Immigration Reform Five Years Later"—CPHS143-02-08, 1. Theodore Martin Hesburgh Papers (PHS), University of Notre Dame Archives (UNDA), Notre Dame, IN 46556.

45. Hesburgh, "Immigration Reform Five Years Later"—CPHS143-02-08, 2.

46. Hesburgh, "Immigration Reform Five Years Later"—CPHS143-02-08, 1.

CHAPTER 7

1. James R. Brockman, *Romero: A Life* (Maryknoll, NY: Orbis, 2005), 47.

2. Brockman, *Romero*, 47.

3. Joseph B. Frazier, *El Salvador Could Be Like That: A Memoir of War, Politics, and Journalism from the Front Row of the Last Bloody Conflict of the U.S.-Soviet Cold War* (Ojai, CA: Karina Library, 2012), 110–11.

4. Brockman, *Romero*, 44.

5. Frazier, *El Salvador*, 111.

6. Paul VI, *Evangelii Nuntiandi* (On Evangelization in the Modern World), Encyclical Letter, December 8, 1975, http://www.vatican.va/content/paul-vi/en/apost_exhortations/documents/hf_p-vi_exh_19751208_evangelii-nuntiandi.html.

7. Óscar Romero, *The Scandal of Redemption: When God Liberates the Poor, Saves Sinners, and Heals Nations* (Walden, NY: Plough, 2018), 13–14.

8. James Lemoyne, "Duarte Accuses a Rightist Leader in Killing of Archbishop in 1980," *New York Times*, November 24, 1987, http://www.nytimes.com/1987/11/24/world/duarte-accuses-a-rightist-leader-in-killing-of-archbishop-in-1980.html.

9. Russell Crandall, *The Salvador Option: The United States in El Salvador, 1977–1992* (New York: Cambridge University Press, 2016), 383.

10. Marcella S. Kreiter, "Notre Dame President to Monitor Salvador Elections," United Press International, March 21, 1982, https://www.upi.com/Archives/1982/03/21/Notre-Dame-president-to-monitor-Salvador-elections/7253385534800/.

11. John E. Newhagen, "U.S. Observers Happy with Turnout," United Press International, March 28, 1982, https://www.upi.com/Archives/1982/03/28/US-observers-happy-with-turnout/6727386139600/.

12. Thomas P. Wyman, "Wrought Profound Changes as President: Hesburgh's Tenure Winds Down at Notre Dame," *Los Angeles Times*, November 23, 1986, https://www.latimes.com/archives/la-xpm-1986-11-23-mn-12658-story.html.

13. Theodore M. Hesburgh, "The Catholic Spirit of Christmas"—CPHS141-01-08, 1–2. Theodore Martin Hesburgh Papers (PHS), University of Notre Dame Archives (UNDA), Notre Dame, IN 46556.

14. Hesburgh, "The Catholic Spirit of Christmas"—CPHS141-01-08, 2.

15. Theodore M. Hesburgh (with Jerry Reedy), *God, Country, Notre Dame* (Notre Dame, IN: University of Notre Dame Press, 1999), 282.

16. Hesburgh (with Reedy), *God, Country, Notre Dame*, 282.

17. Hesburgh (with Reedy), *God, Country, Notre Dame*, 287.

18. Theodore M. Hesburgh, "Untitled Address"—CPHS142-03-01, 7. Theodore Martin Hesburgh Papers (PHS), University of Notre Dame Archives (UNDA), Notre Dame, IN 46556.

19. Hesburgh (with Reedy), *God, Country, Notre Dame*, 288–89.

20. Hesburgh (with Reedy), *God, Country, Notre Dame*, 283.

21. Hesburgh (with Reedy), *God, Country, Notre Dame*, 289.

22. Theodore M. Hesburgh, "The Peace of God"—CPHS141-01-06, 3. Theodore Martin Hesburgh Papers (PHS), University of Notre Dame Archives (UNDA), Notre Dame, IN 46556.

23. Hesburgh, "The Peace of God"—CPHS141-01-06, 3.

24. Hesburgh, "The Peace of God"—CPHS141-01-06, 3.

25. Hesburgh, "The Peace of God"—CPHS141-01-06, 6–7.

26. Hesburgh, "The Peace of God"—CPHS141-01-06, 7.

27. Hesburgh, "The Peace of God"—CPHS141-01-06, 8.

28. Theodore M. Hesburgh, "Untitled Address"—CPHS141-04-05, 1. Theodore Martin Hesburgh Papers (PHS), University of Notre Dame Archives (UNDA), Notre Dame, IN 46556.

29. Hesburgh. "Untitled Address"—CPHS141-04-05, 1.

30. Hesburgh, "Untitled Address"—CPHS141-04-05, 3.

31. Hesburgh, "Untitled Address"—CPHS141-04-05, 7.

32. Hesburgh, "Untitled Address"—CPHS141-04-05, 3.

33. Theodore M. Hesburgh, "Untitled Address"—CPHS141-10-03, 1. Theodore Martin Hesburgh Papers (PHS), University of Notre Dame Archives (UNDA), Notre Dame, IN 46556.

34. Hesburgh, "Untitled Address"—CPHS141-10-03, 3–4.

35. Hesburgh, "Untitled Address"—CPHS141-10-03, 8.

36. Hesburgh, "Untitled Address"—CPHS141-10-03, 11.

37. Hesburgh, "Untitled Address"—CPHS141-10-03, 8.

38. Maritain cited in Hesburgh, "Untitled Address"—CPHS141-10-03, 15.

39. Theodore M. Hesburgh, "Untitled Address"—CPHS141-20-04, 1–2. Theodore Martin Hesburgh Papers (PHS), University of Notre Dame Archives (UNDA), Notre Dame, IN 46556.

40. Theodore M. Hesburgh, "Untitled Address"—CPHS142-06-09, 1. Theodore Martin Hesburgh Papers (PHS), University of Notre Dame Archives (UNDA), Notre Dame, IN 46556.

41. Hesburgh, "Untitled Address"—CPHS142-06-09, 11–12.

42. Theodore M. Hesburgh, "International Fair Play"—CPHS142-06-07, 1. Theodore Martin Hesburgh Papers (PHS), University of Notre Dame Archives (UNDA), Notre Dame, IN 46556.

43. Hesburgh, "International Fair Play"—CPHS142-06-07, 11.

44. Theodore M. Hesburgh, "Untitled Address"—CPHS142-09-04, 3. Theodore Martin Hesburgh Papers (PHS), University of Notre Dame Archives (UNDA), Notre Dame, IN 46556.

45. Maritain cited in Hesburgh, "Untitled Address"—CPHS142-09-04, 14.

46. Hesburgh, "Untitled Address"—CPHS142-09-04, 15.

47. Hesburgh, "Untitled Address"—CPHS142-09-04, 17.

48. Theodore M. Hesburgh, "Universities and the Nuclear Threat"—CPHS142-21-03, 1. Theodore Martin Hesburgh Papers (PHS), University of Notre Dame Archives (UNDA), Notre Dame, IN 46556.

49. Hesburgh, "Universities and the Nuclear Threat"—CPHS142-21-03, 1.

50. Hesburgh, "Universities and the Nuclear Threat"—CPHS142-21-03.

51. Theodore M. Hesburgh, "Eugene Burke Lecture Series-Inaugural Lecture"—CPHS142-22-01. Theodore Martin Hesburgh Papers (PHS), University of Notre Dame Archives (UNDA), Notre Dame, IN 46556.

52. Theodore M. Hesburgh, "Untitled Address"—CPHS142-22-07. Theodore Martin Hesburgh Papers (PHS), University of Notre Dame Archives (UNDA), Notre Dame, IN 46556.

53. Theodore M. Hesburgh, "Untitled Address"—CPHS142-25-02. Theodore Martin Hesburgh Papers (PHS), University of Notre Dame Archives (UNDA), Notre Dame, IN 46556.

54. Theodore M. Hesburgh, Foreword to *Catholics and Nuclear War: A Commentary on "The Challenge of Peace"—The U.S. Catholic Bishops' Pastoral Letter on War and Peace*, ed. Philip J. Murnion (New York: Crossroad, 1983), ix.

55. "Declaration on the Prevention of Nuclear War," in *Catholics and Nuclear War*, 342.

56. Hesburgh, Foreword to *Catholics and Nuclear War*, xiii.

57. Shirley Christian, "Duarte Addresses Notre Dame Class," *New York Times,* May 20, 1985, https://www.nytimes.com/1985/05/20/world/duarte-addresses-norte-dame-class.html.

58. Marlise Simons, "Daughter of Duarte Is Released by Rebels in Complex Exchange," *New York Times,* October 25, 1985, https://www.nytimes.com/1985/10/25/world/daughter-of-duarte-is-released-by-rebels-in-complex-exchange.html.

59. Jon Lee Anderson, "Archbishop Óscar Romero Becomes a Saint, but His Death Still Haunts El Salvador," *New Yorker,* October 22, 2018, https://www.newyorker.com/news/daily-comment/archbishop-oscar-romero-becomes-a-saint-but-his-death-still-haunts-el-salvador.

60. Theodore M. Hesburgh, Foreword to *Duarte: My Life,* by José Napoleón Duarte (New York: G. P. Putnam's Sons, 1986), 9.

CONCLUSION

1. J. Edgar Hoover, Letter to the Honorable Secretary of State [Dean Rusk], February 15, 1962.

2. Clarence H. Kelly, Letter to Jane Dannenhauer, November 18, 1974.

3. Federal Bureau of Investigation (FBI), "Theodore Martin Hesburgh," Washington, DC, June 13, 1991, 9.

4. FBI, "Theodore Martin Hesburgh," June 13, 1991, 11.

5. Theodore M. Hesburgh, *The Theology of Catholic Action* (Notre Dame, IN: Ave Maria Press, 1946), 47–48.

6. Thomas Aquinas, *Summa Theologica,* trans. Fathers of the English Dominican Province (Allen, TX: Christian Classics, 1981), 4:2356–57.

7. Hesburgh, *Theology of Catholic Action,* 65.

8. Hesburgh, *Theology of Catholic Action,* 62–63.

9. Thomas Aquinas, *Summa Theologica,* 4:2138.

10. Hesburgh, *Theology of Catholic Action,* 63.

11. Hesburgh, *Theology of Catholic Action,* 63.

12. Hesburgh, *Theology of Catholic Action,* 63.

13. Thomas Aquinas, *Summa Theologica,* 4:2140.

14. Hesburgh, *Theology of Catholic Action,* 63.

15. Theodore M. Hesburgh, "Science and Modern Man"—CPHS141-07-05, 9. Theodore Martin Hesburgh Papers (PHS), University of Notre Dame Archives (UNDA), Notre Dame, IN 46556.

16. Hesburgh, *Theology of Catholic Action*, 57.

17. Walter Farrell, *A Companion to the Summa IV: The Way of Life* (New York: Sheed & Ward, 1948), 119.

18. Farrell, *Companion*, 119.

19. Farrell, *Companion*, 119.

20. Theodore M. Hesburgh, "Untitled Address"—CPHS141-02-07, 10. Theodore Martin Hesburgh Papers (PHS), University of Notre Dame Archives (UNDA), Notre Dame, IN 46556.

21. Hesburgh, "Untitled Address"—CPHS141-02-07, 10.

22. Etienne Gilson, cited in Theodore M. Hesburgh, "The Function of Theology in the University"—CPHS141-01-04, 13. Theodore Martin Hesburgh Papers (PHS), University of Notre Dame Archives (UNDA), Notre Dame, IN 46556.

INDEX

Index

Index

Knights of Malta, 64
Koch Foods, 92–93
Korea, 32
Ku Klux Klan, 11

Laborem Exercens (On Human
    Work), 103–4
laity (laypersons), 13, 21, 61,
    125–26
Land O' Lakes Statement, 27
Land O' Lakes, WI, xxi, 27
*Last Intellectuals, The: American
    Culture in the Age of Academe*
    (Jacoby, Russell), 7
Leaders, 4, 9, 17, 19, 22. 27, 32, 69,
    70–71, 85, 89–90, 102, 103, 121
Leadership, 2, 39, 47, 61, 70, 86, 99
Le Mans, France, 12
Le Moyne College, 3
Leo XIII, 102–3
Levering, Matthew, 74
liberal arts (liberal education),
    38–39, 41, 90
liberal (political), xix, xxiii, 98
liberation theology, 107
lighthouse (university as a
    lighthouse and a crossroads),
    17–30
literary (arts, man), 35, 131
Little Boy (atomic weapon), 32
logic (logical, logically), 8, 38, 39,
    78, 104, 105, 134
Los Angeles, CA, 69, 85
Los Angeles Times, 2, 109
Love, 1, 17, 50, 54, 58, 63, 74, 95,
    102, 112, 133, 135
Lugo, John, 31–32
Lumen Christi Institute, xx

Lumen Gentium (On the
    Church), 61
Lungren, John C., Jr., xix, xxiii–xxiv
Luther, Martin, 65–67
Lutherans, 67, 79

Machiavelli, Niccoló, 17
malaria, 43
Marion, IN, 45, 58
Maritain, Jacques, xxiii, 23, 54, 57,
    83–84, 101, 116, 119, 133
Maritain, Raïssa, 119
Marxism (Marxists), 107, 121–22
Mary (Dear Mother, Mother of
    God, Virgin), 19, 65
Maryland, 10
Mason-Dixon Line, 45
Mass, 14, 25, 30, 65, 70, 77, 86, 107,
    126, 129–30, 131, 133, 134
Massachusetts Institute of
    Technology (MIT), 37, 42,
    43, 99
materialism, 38, 42
mathematics (mathematical,
    mathematician), 19, 23, 83, 111
Matthew (Gospel of), 101–2, 132
Mazzoli, Romano, 99
McComb, MS, 46, 55
McGee, Tony, 92–93, 105
mediator (mediatorial, mediatory),
    1, 14, 15, 17, 19–22, 24–25,
    26–27, 29–30, 51, 67, 74, 78, 87,
    91, 95, 125–28, 131
mediocre (mediocrity), 20, 133
Mennonites, 79
Merton, Thomas, 72
Mervosh, Sarah, 2
Michael, John, 7
Michigan, 11

Index

Index